Street Kids

Street Kids

by **Larry Cole**

with **Ralph Romero**

Pauli Vizzio

Eddie Burgos

Charlie Galletti

Grossman Publishers   *New York*   1970

Published by Grossman Publishers, Inc.
125A East 19th Street, New York, N. Y. 10003
Published simultaneously in Canada by
Fitzhenry and Whiteside, Ltd.
Manufactured in the United States.
Library of Congress Catalogue Card Number: 78–121374
First Printing

For Michelle
who loves the best
the flowers
cracking through
   the sidewalk

Introduction

Writing a book about street kids is like trying to describe a volcano. There's really no beginning or end. You can describe the eruptions, but it is difficult to describe the energy of the force below, the power that hasn't happened yet. Whatever you describe is only what you choose to look at, never all there is.

The life of the streets is volcanic and its kids stand out as its energy, its subterranean power. But to write only of the eruptions, the surface expressions, is to miss the essence of street life. I am, instead, writing about people and about myself. And I hope that by this particular accumulation of impressions and ideas you will get a sense of the power underneath; the flux, the destruction, and the brilliance, the lack of definition that defines the madness of the street.

I came into the streets as an outsider. A transplant who, with my wife Michelle, found myself looking for life where so many find death. It was 1962 and with all our angry energy built up by years of pointlessness in college and graduate schools, Michelle and I found ourselves drawn to New York's Lower East Side. We agreed in our love for kids. Our experiences with New York street kids, while finishing graduate school in psychology, just made that love impossible to put aside. A strong mixture of anger and love. It boiled out into an adventure we are still on. An adventure called LEAP.

Starting in a storefront on East Sixth Street on Manhattan's Lower East Side, the Lower Eastside Action Project (LEAP) was born with some simple guidelines: that kids and adults can help each other if they want—that nobody who's working with kids knows what they're doing—that the street kids we had met had more integrity than all the university people we had so long suffocated with.

From that rigid base, an organization grew without our really knowing it. Without knowing the first little bit about fund raising, New York City corruption, organization building, New York City corruption, ghetto education, police hostility, New York City corruption, or the supposed dangers of working in this "high crime area," LEAP just happened. A little at a time.

With the kind of incredible naiveté it takes to begin such an impossibility, we opened up a storefront with money we made at other jobs (Michelle as Assistant to the Fashion Editor of *Playboy*, and me as a researcher for the National Institute for Mental Health), and for the first few months I played judo with the group of kids who, through their own curiosity, and after a week of security checking, just walked in one day and stayed for years.

Introduction

Judo turned to coffee and coffee turned to involvement into the lives of those first thirty-five kids. We just became each other's family and the organization stuff that followed was just to get the family where it wanted to go. We had, in the words of Dr. Harold Greenwald, a New York psychoanalyst, "the only really existential organization I have ever seen."

Over the years, developed completely out of donations from private foundations and individuals, LEAP has become a kind of idea-clearinghouse, an intergeneracial innovation for the many kids and adults who have used it. It has been a community organization, a newspaper publisher, a tutorial project, home, children's rights group, law office, medical center, center of controversy, wedding chapel, dance hall, and traveling caravan.

It is an experimental high school, kid-run community in and out of the city, a residence, and a media explosion. I have no idea where it is going. I try to let go and trust it.

And so I write, as participant observer, of the people and conditions I met and still meet as part of this intergeneracial thing. This LEAP. But this isn't a book about LEAP. It is about the kids I have met and that you should meet. I tell you a little of LEAP so you can know my vantage point and most of all so you will know that while I am an outsider I am not a tourist.

I hope the libraries catalog this book under Conservation. For just as exploitation and mindlessness have created the present crisis in our ecology, just as unprotected animals and forests are now in danger of extinction, the kids of the streets are being forever lost to disease, drugs, and defeat.

Introduction

And so these impressions. Polaroids, you might say. Unprocessed views of and by kids who have been hidden from America's consciousness, but not its destructiveness. Pictures of the volcano by some cliff dwellers.

lsc
New York City
April 1970

Contents

Illustrations by Carlos Toledo and Mike Gonzalez. Photographs by Ralph Romero, Pauli Vizzio, and Eddie Burgos.

Street Kids

The street: an underview

Street warfare, drugs, baptisms, dances, courts, overdoses, evictions, weddings, and wakes. Kids who sleep on rooftops, on subways, in doorways, with faggots or, somehow, not at all. Kids who hate, cling, doubt, search, punch, joke, die, and (rarely) cry. Kids who smile that funny little smile. Kids who knew that the poverty program would fail but never knew why.

Supersaturated, social-worked, skeptical kid walks in and asks "Who the hell are you anyway?" And you know from that matador pose and pout that you are going to see this kid again. And again. You know you'll be asked slowly into his unbelievable life. You can flip a coin whether you'll matter. Even odds become overwhelmingly positive. You answer back a wiseass answer, knowing it means soon acceptance of the impossible.

Here it is. Flash. One kid . . .

One kid? What the hell difference does it make, one kid?

Okay. How about this? We'll make it two kids. A 100 per cent increase over the original proposal. Let's see now.

Here it is. At $50 a day for a kid's detention, and $15,000 for a kid's year in the Job Corps, times the number of the poverty program's immobile social workers, times the square root of $100,000 per junkie, all multiplied by the $350,000 for a dead Viet Cong and divided by the gross national product, these two kids, to make them real breathing, voting, taxpaying members of the working force (throw in opening their eyes to their own magnificence and independence) will cost you . . . five million dollars a year.

Give y'a thousand. First write a proposal. Write it in triplicate. We'll stick some pins in it and see if it floats. Tone you down a little. Jack you up. Then we'll give y'a thousand. Builds the character.

Okay. We're through that. Take the bread and split, two kids richer.

All of this is what we'll walk through. What I'll fumble for words for to bridge the static barrier and raise some money for more kids. For LEAP.

Here is living as outsider inside. What a hundred pouting smiles have led me through. Stumbling, falling, bruised and stepping barefoot on the sharp edges of fallen glass idols. That damn haunting slum kid smile. These kids are going to get me all involved.

The first stop is the second, the forty-ninth, and the third. It is a picture. Conglomerate of all of this, and more . . .

Storefronts, basements, tenements, alleys, schoolyards, precinct houses, lawyers' offices, hospital waiting rooms, principals' offices, and street corners. The acid smell of tenement hallways, the hard, careless benches of Children's Court, the falling plaster of decaying apartments, and the sick green walls of indifferent Emergency Rooms.

Waiting.

Phone calls at 4:00 A.M. after crises at 2:00. Sleeping in court before the case is called. Senseless man in black robes under In God We Trust, telling sixteen-year-old Puerto Rican kid spic spic spic spic. Justice. Equal justice. Black kids get the same.

Kid with head opened up by frightened civil servant doing his duty. Kid with stitched lip cracked by cop and stitched without benefit of anaesthetic. Be nice, kid.

Kids without food, without clothes, and without teeth. Sick kids, sick with rickets, brain tumors, ulcers, and forgottenness. Kids who have seen a doctor only during their brief moment of birth and don't remember their unteeveed coming out party.

Kids who have come to expect adults to exploit them. Their pride, their defenses, and their bodies. Kids who couldn't learn to read because they couldn't see. And nobody knew. And they weren't telling.

Kids who knew that California was in Jersey. Kids in public school for eight years who couldn't tell time. Kids who never knew their birthdays. Kids who never had a present or a kiss. . . . Kids who didn't give a shit for you and all your lies.

Kids stoned on glue, on goofballs, Carbona, and wine. The glassy-eyed indifference of the graduate to heroin. Shit. H. Junk. Dope.

Tears. Fearful mothers intimidated and disgraced

by welfare workers poking through dirty laundry bags. Welfare police in midnight raids catching little girl mothers unsafe even in bed.

Kangaroo courts in public housing evicting families whose children break the law. The law. Unmarried mothers of breathing children being refused a place on the housing list. People with no place to live. People living where people shouldn't.

A street rumble out of nowhere. Kids with guns, chains, and knives slashing and shooting other kids who can't say, either, why it is happening. Kids who have been offered a choice. Kill each other. Be killed. Kill yourself. Cops stand and watch the spics and boogies fight. Rooting for both sides to lose.

Kids who live by pure chance and through the strangest of coincidence. Kids who know nothing of foundations, the poverty program, social work training, or teachers' demands because they can't read *The New York Times*. Kids who are too young to be dropouts and too old for Head Start.

Kids who are unimpressed by politicians or other superstars. Kids who are strangely unaffected by job training programs or addiction scare shots in Health class. Kids who think social workers are schmucks when they don't know that smell is pot. Grass, baby. Smoke. Get a nice head. . . .

Go to court, rap to the police, intimidate the bureaucrat, and watch your language with teachers and foundation people. Tell people enough so they know you know, but not the truth, the whole truth. It will turn them off. No one likes the story about the kid whose convulsions made the gym coach laugh. They don't like the punch line that a year of laughing made his brain tumor terminal. . . . Dick and Jane never had a little brother with a bleeding ulcer.

It is too dark and too crazy to be the Twilight Zone.

No one harps on death or pain. It's yours, baby, you keep it. Kid runs in . . . "guy got shot on Third Street with a big .38. Like in the movies. Bam. Pow. Guy fell over in the street with two big holes in his back. Man, that was boss. I likeded it." Play with that one a while. He likeded it.

If it was his brother, honor would have dictated action. In any case, feelings—feeeeellllliiinnnggggssss —were not involved. Do what you gotta do. Get the hell out.

Kids beat up bums. Yeah. They really do it. They set them on fire. Like scarecrows. They're not people, man. Fire hurts. Get that match away from my ear. Help! Somebody help! Kids running down and away from the Bowery hotels. Ghost of Christmas future. Ghost of Christmas father. Run like hell. Run. Run. Run.

See Frankie run. Run Frankie run. Run out the door of school when they've got you down as present. Beat it to the bag of glue and get away. Up high. You can't read the label that says glue can kill you. You are a disruptive child. You are disadvantaged. You are a non-intellectual. You are delinquent, or if you're not delinquent, you're predelinquent. Everyone has a label, a reason, and ready-made absolution for their failure to teach you what you will need to grow up. You don't know when September is. You don't know that the guy who discovered America sailed from Spain. You don't know how to read your own name.

Your teacher is the cheerleader of mockery. You

are a fourteen-year-old failure. How the hell can that happen? Hide out. Sniff. Stay away from your mom and the truant officer. After school go home. Grab a bean and cut out. Be cool. Hang with the guys. You don't have to tell each other anything.

Clang on the garbage can and watch. You have disturbed the dinner of three brown things. Rats. They run across the sidewalk and into the basement. Out of sight. You wonder what they're doing. You hear stories. Mothers tell you.

Little girl baby woke up with a foot-long rat eating her nose. And the kids grow up forgetting these nightmare nights. Forgetting. Like forgetting when the apartment burned with all their new and only clothes. With all their mother's non-welfare prided furniture. Like forgetting when their stomach pains began. Forgetting when your mother smiled shy and obvious smiles at the fat bastard landlord who never gave you heat. Rent every week. Overcharges from the grocer for the privilege of credit. Up the prices every month comes the welfare check. Forget it, baby. Forget it. Just don't clang on the garbage can, don't play with matches, stay away from junkies, go to church and forget it.

You begin to wonder the things you take for granted. Bed. A meal. Health. Love. Alternatives. You have always had all of these. Now each becomes a treasure. Bed. A clean bed with fresh cool sheets. Electric blanket in the winter. Foam rubber mattress. Stretch out, spread-eagle, dig it, it's yours.

Bed. A mattress on a broken folding cot, covered with the presents of little brother who used it during its daylight emptiness as a playpen up from momma's feet. Find a blanket if you can and sleep with your clothes on. Sweaters. Woolen scarves. Get the hell up and out of bed early and get somewhere it's warm.

Meals. Hustle a bag of potato chips. A soda. That's dinner, baby. And breakfast and lunch.

That's no way for kids to grow up. What the hell they doing with my money building World's Fairs when these kids are hungry? What the hell they shooting off those big missile fireworks when one of my kids does without five-dollar medicine? What the hell they up to sending congressmen to Europe when my kid never been past the Bronx? What the hell they teaching in their social work schools sitting behind their half-partitioned foggy glass walls when this kid wants someone to pick him up and squeeze him? How many times you walk in and see a social worker holding a kid? A big ugly kid. Wrestling. It's okay, Mr. Socialworker. He won't think you're a faggot if you hug him.

Walk the streets at night. Nothing open for kids. All the big-mouthed people have gone home to the hills. Rap all day about poverty wars and then cut out at sundown when the troops are on the street. Weekends? Forget it. When you're in trouble, kid, just run like hell and hide.

Kids in candy stores, on the streets, and in hallways. Kids sitting on stoops watching fixed channel action. Kids in basements with glue bags and in playgrounds with half-filled wine bottles. Goofing.

No place to go. "Hey man, got a nickel?" Move off the corner when the cop comes around. How come with all this poverty money in the neighborhood a kid has no place to go at night. When he's out. Like it or not, he's out. And no place to go. A strange absence of legitimate activities. Stoop sitting. The corner. The hallway.

In and out of fast illegalities. Snatching handbags. Smoking pot. Sometimes just rapping to the chicks in the projects. The kids from the housing projects. They have no place to go either. You just mill around. Waiting. For nothing.

You are in the constant sight of the law. Since you have no place to go you stand out in the open. You and the law always looking each other square in the face. When something happens near you, man, you're in it. Like it or not. You are a part of the scene. You will get busted for just being. You are too close to the action not to get pulled along. Almost everyone has a record. If you don't have a record you're a freak. You know the odds keep building up against you. You know you'll get busted sooner or later. Like it or not, you are part of the scene.

It is a scene of multilanguage music straining down from fire escapes onto streets and sidewalks filled with dirt and the smells of cooped up animals walking on leashes trained to relieve themselves in the gutter or on the tires of parked cars. Cats playing with the leashed dogs, taunting them from under cars and behind garbage cans. The smell from the street rises to meet the soot and noises descending. Crumpled newspapers, beer cans, and bottles lie in the street moved only by cars and occasional winds. Kids darting in and out of the cars, dodging moving traffic, broken bottles and shit. Running in this field as if it were a fairytale meadow. Playing.

They play without caution or reserve. Boxes become cars. Garbage can tops become shields. Truck tires become amusement park rides. The street is made to work. It is thoroughfare, playground, trading floor, theater, battlefield, ballroom, boardwalk, garbage dump, parking lot, convention hall, game preserve, mortuary, boxing arena, and circus. It is a world, total, bounded by two avenues. It has its own candy store, market, barber, shoe repair, drug store, cop, pusher, and politician. The block doesn't need the world at all. And its kids become part of its self-containedness. Their chauvinism bounded by two avenues.

A littered minefield nestled safely away from affluence. Subways don't come here. Taxis don't stop. Everyone knows all that, and it's okay until you need a way in. Or out. The things that happen here stay here. No one sees the whole show without a reserved seat. Recommended for mature audiences only.

A fat lady comes out of nowhere wearing nothing but panties. On Avenue C at 10:00 P.M. wearing nothing but panties. Beating a bum with a piece of board. A small crowd gathers. Kids laugh, others walk past, not caring. Someone calls the cops. Too much noise.

On Avenue D, nearly at the same time, a guy jumps off the roof of the projects. Ten floors to the bottom. Swing out open windows crash as his body falls on its way to the litter in the street.

Kid runs up and says "Hey, what's a suislide? Some guy did a suislide."

The cops come and join the crowd cheering the near-naked fat lady. She has stopped being a nuisance. She is the fat lady. It is a side show.

The guy on Avenue D died, doing his jump without a net.

Study kids' faces and eyes through all of this. Try to find some measure of reaction. Something to measure your own sense of reality by. Is this really happening? These are kids and they see it all. Is it happening to them?

Look and look hard. You see nothing. It is not happening to them. It is Channel 14 that comes on when it's ready. It's you that turns on and off.

The kids are turned off. They're turned off to death, disease, school, destruction, adults, politics, rent strikes, reading, jobs, promises, cleaner streets, junkies, air pollution, high prices and low rents, principals, cops, social workers, priests, guidance counselors, welfare workers, building inspectors, mayors, and Reform Democrats. They are, above all, turned off to themselves. They have nothing to lose.

Depression. Try to find words to put feelings in boxes. WHAT DO I DO WITH THIS? I see it all. Feel the sticky dirty heat in the summer. Smell the same smells. But I am not of this place and this confused outrage is my proof of birth.

I see a cop punch a fourteen-year-old kid in the mouth and push him into a hallway to finish the job. I see a car drop a package of heroin to a local pusher in front of fifty people. I see someone breaking a car windshield with a garbage can. I see a judge read *The Daily News* while a trial is in session. I see a stabbing where people cheer. And all the time, I watch the kids' faces. It is not happening to them.

I go on with my two kids, now two hundred, then fifty, then a hundred more. Go on and finally wonder why we are walking together at all. Who is guide and who is guided? Who has what to learn from whom? Who is educated? Who is expert?

I learn, slowly, to shut up and listen. To forget Sigmund Freud and Weschsler-Bellevue. To forget statistics, prognoses, and professional distance. To move away from the holiness of self-fulfilling prophecies and toward the callous business of hustling doctors, teachers, dentists, lawyers and others, like myself, still untilted. I learn what my years of schooling never taught. I learn, slowly, to see, to feel, and to act.

Charlie A. goes to school

Charlie at fifteen was a fast-talking, hustling kid who was in and out of trouble. His main interests were cars and girls, in that order. He hardly ever went to school. When he did this is what he encountered. The "CG" following his class stands for "Career Guidance"—a special program for pre-diagnosed dropouts. It works—most of the kids in CG classes do drop out. It worked for Charlie too. Six months after this was mechanically copied, Charlie was out of school and shooting dope.

JHS 71   Charles A.
Class 9 C.G.

List Pie filling crust
12 peaches   1 box pie crust mix
2-½ cups sugar

½ cups flower
1 stick butter

1 turn the oven on 350
2 Mix pie crust (?) mix with water and rolled it out
3 butter the pie pan place the crust inside
4 wash the peaches peel them slice them
5 Mix 3 cups of water with sugar and flower Heat in
   pan until almost thick

How to make a telegraph

List
Wood BATTERIES
NAIL TIN
WIRE

Samson

*H*is real name was Pedro, Peter, but he was called Samson because of his super strength. At the height of the teen gang era of the late '50's, Samson commanded over a thousand young Puerto Rican, black, and even a few white Lower East Side street kids. The city, threatened by the existence of the street gangs and not imaginative or visionary enough to see their constructive potential, set out to destroy them with a typical disregard for the balance of nature. As usual, the city fathers offered nothing to replace what they were taking away and thousands of displaced kids were suddenly left without the family surrogate the gang offered. Drugs rushed into the vacuum.

Samson found himself leader of nothing. Just as the Biblical Samson had his strength taken away being seduced by a woman bent on clipping his hair, our Puerto Rican Samson was dumped from field marshal to displaced person after a similar seduction by the social workers of New York City. In both cases strength was the threat. In both cases greater exploitation of the already oppressed would be the result.

Samson bounced around in the few years after the gangs were subverted away, still keeping the fantasy of his Latin Crowns alive by meeting with his boys on the street corners and talking about the old days. The wars. The victories. The glory. The defeats. He tried at first to muscle any of his boys who moved toward drugs but the lure was too strong and the numbers too many. More of his boys drifted into dope.

I met Samson at the tail end of his gang leadership. I had never before seen a leader whose strengths and function were so obvious. He was physically strong but not a bully. In fact, he underplayed his physical superiority with the modesty of a champion. He was shrewd. He thought fast and on his feet. He did not speak well, but he spoke with authority. With wisdom even. And everyone listened.

He was a consummate diplomat. He was arbitrator to some of the most complex territorial and jurisdictional negotiations, always with explosive adversaries on both sides. One guy came to one such meeting with a machine gun. And Samson settled things, usually without so much as raising his voice.

One early morning, Samson was arrested. The police came to his house and took him to jail. They said he had been identified by a neighborhood storekeeper who had just been held up at gun point. While awaiting trial, his bail was set at ten thousand dollars.

Now no one had ten thousand dollars lying around for Samson's bail. No one even had the bail premium and the bond security needed for collateral. Most of his friends were just making money for rent. So Samson sat in jail, not convicted, not even tried. Just accused. And poor.

I got permission to see him and he leveled. He knew who it was who pulled the job. The guys outside had gotten word to him. But it wasn't him. He was home and in bed at the time. And besides, wasn't he too smart to pull a *gies* (job) right down the block from where he lived. Yes, he was.

The Latin Crowns mobilized, many of them coming back from their first affair with drugs when they heard of Samson's troubles. Quickly, they uncovered facts that the police could never come near. They got people to talk. They solved the crime. Only trouble was the courts were a few miles south and it was *those* judges who had Samson locked up. The Latin Crowns said it clear that it would be a violation of every rule of the streets to ever cooperate with *them*. Even if it meant getting their own boy out of jail. They were going to have to catch the guy and get him to rat on himself. They would give him at least one other choice and they felt certain what his decision would be. They came close. Just as they almost had him nailed, he left for Puerto Rico. Samson stayed locked up. The grocery man would still identify him as the culprit. There was a slight resemblance. Enough for a man with a gun in his ribs to make an honest mistake. Samson stood to be convicted for a crime he didn't commit and armed robbery brought a sure three years.

By a strange set of coincidences a lawyer walked into LEAP just about that time and offered his services. He was an uptown lawyer with a big-time law firm. Everyone liked him and trusted him even if his name was Galligan. His LEAP baptism was Samson's case.

For three months Arthur J. Galligan went into court, first trying to get the bail reduced (he got it reduced to five thousand—still no good), then trying to shake the district attorney's faith in his case. He spoke at length to Samson over and over again trying to make sure in his own mind that he was telling the truth. Samson's stories checked and crosschecked. The guys outside told their stories and they checked. The real holdup man was a guy named Red and he was in Puerto Rico. But that was privileged information.

After four months of bugging the D.A. and especially because here was this big-time lawyer making all this fuss over a Puerto Rican gang kid, the city finally agreed to a lie detector test. On the day before what would have been his fifth month in jail, awaiting trial, Samson walked out free. His lie detector test was passed and the D.A. let him go. He was in jail for five months, suffering the indignities and cruelty that go with being an inmate of New York's prison system, had been branded a gunman by the press and the older neighbors, had drained the meager resources of his family who found it difficult to raise the weekly carfare for their visits to their son, and was, all at once, found innocent by a machine, all before any kind of trial. But Samson's story only begins here.

In the last few days of his imprisonment he had witnessed a death. He said, when he got out, that he had been a witness to murder. And even though he had nothing to gain and everything to lose, even though it meant risking the wrath of the system that had just had him wrongfully locked up for five months of hell, he felt it was his duty to tell what he had seen. He was still Samson.

"There was this kid thrown into the cell one night and he was bleeding pretty bad from his head. It turned out he was this Jewish kid and he just robbed some liquor store or something and the cops caught him and beat hell out of him with their clubs. Anyway, they threw him into the cell and he didn't talk much. He just cried and screamed for a doctor. He was vomiting and screaming and crying so I made some noise for the guard to come and take the kid to the doctor. Then everybody started calling for the guard to come.

"Finally the guard came and told the kid to shut up or he'd get it even worse. He said that the doctor would look at him the next day.

"We didn't hear much noise from him after a while and we all thought he went to sleep. Another guy shook him to see if he was okay and the Jewish kid fell off his bed. He was dead.

"Everybody called the guard and told him and the guard, he just smiled and walked away. They left the kid's body lying there for eight hours. Then they tried to get everyone to sign these statements saying that the kid died while they were bringing him in. Most everybody who had to do time in that place signed. I didn't sign nothin'."

Looking back to that day's newspaper, we found a small article about the death of the boy Samson saw die. The newspaper article said the boy died on the way to the hospital after injuries suffered at the scene of the attempted robbery. The New York City Department of Correction lie had become the only available story. And Samson, a Puerto Rican kid who never had much happy contact with Jews, saw it as his responsibility to set the record straight.

He took his story to James Wechsler of *The New York Post* whose column is the only consistent voice of the poor and powerless of New York and Wechsler told it straight in his column. He demanded an investigation and there was one. The results of that investigation never made headlines, but Samson's risk had caused the Department of Correction to increase its medical coverage and to mandate medical examination prior to a prisoner's being locked up. Maybe other kids, Jewish or Puerto Rican or whatever, would be saved by this simple administrative change.

Maybe is maybe, but for Samson trouble was coming for sure.

His name was in the papers about the kid who died. He was a kind of hero for a little while . . . the kind local officials just don't like . . . the kind who rats on the system. Besides, he had beaten the robbery rap with a fancy lawyer and a lie detector and made the arresting cops look bad. He was getting to be famous for telling the world outside what kids had for so long kept to themselves: that the system of justice, especially for them, was a sham. He was positively dangerous. Other kids began telling their stories and people started listening.

Kids on the block, Latin Crowns and others, began organizing again. Only this time they were organizing around issues of police crime. They reported cases where kids were beaten up by police nightsticks for drinking in hallways. They reported cases of cops drinking in those same hallways. They picketed an uptown precinct when the Puerto Rican Boy of the Year was killed by an off-duty patrolman's bullet. And they did this all around their leader, Samson, who was once only a local hero but was now, for them, a media hero. A culture hero in their own *barrio*.

Kids were keeping Galligan busy with facts of police misconduct. Galligan, in turn, made formal charges to the Police Department's Civilian Complaint Review Board, a group of policemen who reviewed charges brought against other policemen. The Review Board, in turn, was busy checking out the facts and holding hearings. The local cops, in their turn, were called down to these hearings, usually on their days off, to answer the charges.

Samson, also in turn, was picked up, threatened, and knocked around by the police four times in the next two months. No charges were filed, he was just "picked up for questioning," or was the victim of "unknown assailants." One night, nearly three months after his release from jail on the mistaken identity thing, he was hit hard. A group of three police detectives broke down the door to his apartment and turned the place inside out. They broke and turned over furniture, tore mattresses, spilled food and milk containers, and emptied closets and dressers onto the floor. Then they told him that he would have to pay them three hundred dollars by 2:00 A.M. that night (this was at 10:00 P.M.) or they would plant some dope in his apartment and bust him for possession. They would meet him in front of a local bar.

In a case like this, Samson was not about to call the police. He knew that even if he showed them the torn-up apartment they would say it was done by burglars. He knew also there was no way they would believe (publicly, anyway) that other cops were trying to shake him down. So he had his choice. Three hundred dollars or another stint in jail. And it was only a maybe that he would get another crack at the lie detector. After all, he was now the local troublemaker. No matter that the facts his boys came up with were, for the most part, true. No matter that their cop clean-up efforts had moved them back to life and given their gang a more positive direction than the abundantly available heroin. Samson was the leader of a bunch of spic troublemakers who had the chutzpah to take policemen's badge numbers when these policemen broke the law. Samson the subversive.

But Samson was still Samson. He called me and we got to the Police Commissioner's Office and finally woke up an assistant district attorney who had a particular dislike for crooked cops. In a matter of a half hour, the Police Commissioner's Confidential Investigation Unit, a group of honest cops who, like Elliot Ness's men were untouchable, and called, by their brothers in blue, "shoeflies," were on the scene. They apparently had heard this story before. What all the detective stories call the *"modus operandi"* was familiar. They gave Samson some marked money, and staked out the area around the bar.

But corrupt cops have a counterintelligence force. When the Police Commissioner's shoeflies move, the cops on the take or on the hustle know where they go. Somehow.

The shakedown men never showed up. He waited until three and went to bed. That was the end of that.

But for Samson, it was only the beginning of bigger and better things to come. During the next two months he was arrested twice on drug charges. Pot, they said. Two sales. On one of the dates of one of the alleged sales he was with me nearly one hundred miles from New York. In each of the two cases he was re-leased on small bail only to be rearrested after the first and stopped and frisked on the street almost daily after the second. Samson got the message. He was marked.

I didn't know what to tell him. What the hell do you say? "Hey, you did a nice thing for that dead Jew-ish kid, and you know, virtue is its own reward." Or, "Hey, your boys are back together again, isn't it worth what you're going through." No. Not even as a joke. Samson had put his ass on the line one way or another, he knew he was going to pay. There was nothing to say about it. Nothing to do but wait.

The next few arrests made bail impossible. During the next year he spent more time inside awaiting trial than he spent free. With all this smoke, the harassed judges who saw his record sheet at the turnstile trials thought in their fleeting glance at still another young faceless Puerto Rican standing before them, with all this smoke, there must be fire. So for some charge or another, Samson got time. He finally made it to prison for real, not for lack of bail. And by the time he got out most of his boys who were still alive were strung out on dope.

So what the hell. There are some things that beat even Samsons, and the next I heard from him he was beaten. We met one morning for breakfast and I almost didn't recognize him.

"I want to get the hell off these drugs," he said, "and I want t' get off that goddamn street." Two days later he was off to Synanon in California. But I knew he'd be back.

The birds and bees

I remember when I heard a conversation with one of the teachers in school and a little girl 12 years old.

Girl: Hey, I got to go to the bathroom!

Teacher: Go right ahead.

The girl ran to the bathroom. All of a sudden she started screaming and crying. The teacher ran to the bathroom, and a lot of students.

Teacher: What's wrong with you?

Girl: I-I-I-I-I don't know, and I'm bleeding. Am I going to die? What's wrong with me?

Teacher: Let me take a look.

Didn't your mother ever tell you something like this was supposed to happen?

Girl: No. I don't know why everything always happens to me.

Teacher: You have nothing to worry about.

Girl: Nothing to worry about! I'm bleeding to death. What should I do?

Teacher: Don't worry. Looks like I have to tell you about the birds and bees.

Everybody go back to your classes. Everything is alright.

Girl: Hold on to me.

Teacher: Sure, sure, let's go into my office.

You had a period.

Girl: A period! What the hell is that?

Teacher: At your age and on, all girls have what you call a period.

Girl: Go on.

Teacher: All girls get their period. The reason is that the woman's body has to be prepared in case the girl conceives a baby. The body stores up blood in case a baby is conceived; if so then the blood is used to nourish the baby. But, if the egg in your uterus isn't fertilized then the blood isn't needed so it drops out.

Girl: Thanks a lot, I think I understand now. Would you give me a pass to go home.

Teacher: Well I really can't, but you go down to the dean and tell him what happened.

Girl: Do I have to tell him what happened to me?

Teacher: Well, let me see what I can do.

Girl: Thanks a lot.

The dean of boys

I remember when I was in Public School, Junior High School 60. And it was very warm outside.

It was 12:45 in the afternoon and we just got in school after we finished a punch ball game. I always liked the school, but to this day the teachers just don't understand. There are 7 periods in a whole day, and I was going to my 6th period class when the Dean of Boys just grabbed me.

Dean: What the hell are you doing in the halls?

Paul: I was—. He cut me off.

Dean: Everytime I see you, you're always roaming around the halls or looking for trouble.

Paul: I was just going to my class, and by the way, it's not late anyway.

Dean: Just get in class.

I got in class and everything was cool.

Now I am going to my last period class and I can't wait for it to finish, because I want to get out and mess around outside (so does everybody). My last period class is Spanish and I am supposed to be on my last year in Spanish, anyway that's what my teacher said.

I don't know what's going on in this classroom, so I am kinda not interested in what's going on. I tried to tell the principal my problem but he said, "Paul, your records say you're on your last year of Spanish, and if you want to pass and get out of this school you'd better do your best."

Then I told my guidance counselor. "What's happening?" I said, "I didn't even take my regents, I didn't take no kind of test in that class, so what are you people trying to pull."

Teacher: If your records say you passed, what can I do. You could get dropped into a lower class, but you won't get no credit for it.

Paul: So then what's the use? Aw man, forget it. Then he said, "It's up to you Paul."

This was almost in the beginning of the year that I brought this up.

Anyway, I was in my Spanish class at my usual seat in back of the classroom. I went to my seat and tore out a piece of paper and took out a pen and started drawing. Just then somebody hit me with a piece of paper in the front of my head. I sort of saw who threw it, so when the teacher turned his back I rolled up a piece of paper and hit the guy who hi me. The teacher didn't see anything, but that started everything.

Mostly everybody in the class was making paper planes and everytime the teacher turned his back there were planes all over.

Teacher: What in the world is going on here?

I started laughing because this really gets him up tight and he lets everybody know it. So naturally he calls me and says "Get out of here." Then Charlie started laughing and he sent both of us out, and sure enough, there was the Dean of Boys standing right there.

Dean: "Get in my office." As we got into his office he separated us. "Charlie get in the corner over there, and YOU get in this corner."

Paul: Mr. Dean, aren't you going to ask us what happened in there?

Dean: I know what happened, now turn your heads against the wall.

As we turned our heads the Dean was staring at Charlie and Charlie was staring at the Dean and that seemed very funny to me because we were smiling, and then all of a sudden Charlie got serious and this made me laugh. The Dean now left Charlie and came to me.

Dean: What's so funny Paul?

Paul: Ha, nothing.

Dean: SMACK. Don't laugh in my face!

Paul: You mother——. BAM. I punched him in the face and threw the chair in his way.

Charlie: Good shit Pauli.

Paul: Come on, let's get the fuck out of this place.

As I was leaving I said, "You didn't realize why I was laughing and you hit me, so I didn't realize why you hit me and I hit you back."

As soon as I hit the Dean he sat down and looked shocked. After that I left school and didn't come back for like 2 weeks, and when I came back he saw me and

I saw him and neither one of us said a word, so even now we still don't know each other.

The school never takes an interest in trying to understand each other.

The pigeon coop

Me and my friend Butch had a pigeon coop on top of a roof and we needed some tin to cover the coop for the winter. So the next morning I went to Butch's house.

Paul: Is Butch home?

Mother: Yes, come in. He's in the bathroom. Why don't you wait out here.

Paul: Thank you.

Butch: Yo! Paul, what's happening?

Paul: I don't know, you going down?

Butch: Yeah! Lay up. Mom, I'll see you later, I'm going down.

Mother: You coming back for supper?

Butch: Yeah, I'll be home.

Paul: Let's go try and find some tin.

Butch: For what?

Paul: For the pigeon coop.

Butch: Alright, but where?

Paul: Let's go to any old buildings.

Butch: Which one?

Paul: Well, let's go to Seventh Street, maybe we'll find a little over there.

Butch: How the fuck are we going to get in this building?

Paul: Let's go through the backyard.

Butch: Okay.

Paul: Watch you don't get cut, there's a lot of glass laying all over.

Butch: I know, I could see.

Paul: Ah! Fuck you then.

Butch: Look on the fire escape, there's a little pigeon coop.

Paul: Maybe there's birds in there.

Butch: Wait: let's get that piece of tin right there.

Paul: Grab it man, I want to see what's up there.

Butch: That building looks condemned anyway, I'm going up too.

Paul: There isn't anything in here.

Butch: How the fuck did you get up there?

Paul: Climb on the telephone wires and pull yourself up.

Butch: Shit, are you crazy?

Paul: Come on, it's only on the 2nd floor.

Butch: Damn! I ain't going down that way. Let's go through the window and down the stairs.

Paul: Come on, I'll open the window.

Butch: Oh shit, somebody lives here, look at the baby.

Paul: Come on Butch, let's get the fuck out of here.

Butch: Come on.

As he turned his back toward the window a man jumped out and grabbed him.

Paul: Butch, run!

Butch: I can't, the fucking guy's got a knife.

Butch: Come in here Pauli. He said he's going to kill me if you don't come in.

Paul: Let him go, I'm coming.

Man: Get inside, go on. My fucking house has been robbed three times already, now I caught you guys. You kids are going to feel sorry.

Paul & Butch: But we didn't even know people lived here.

Man: Shut up! And don't try and get away. I'm a karate instructor and a track team teacher.

Me and Butch didn't say a word because we thought this guy was crazy. He looked like a junkie, a dirty hippie, or a plain nut. Me and Butch was thinking the same thing, because he kept looking at me and I kept looking at him.

I was saying to myself "Damn! Everything always happens to me. I hope he calls the *cops*. I'd rather let the cops take me than this fucking guy." Finally he goes to the phone and makes a call.

Then the fucking guy says to us "Don't worry, it won't be long now."

Me and Butch shook, man. I was shitting in my pants and I could imagine Butch. The cops walked in 3 minutes later. Boy, I was sure glad to see them (for the first time). Anyway, they took us out of there and into the police car. They rode us around the block and said "He told me what happened, so don't go back over there." They told us to go home.

Butch: What the fuck happened? Why did he call the cops if he didn't want anything to happen to us?

Paul: I don't know, but I'm sure glad.

After the movies

I remember when me and a few guys and girls went to a movie. It was on a Friday night. After the movie was over everybody started to bullshit about the flick. It was this, it was that, and the best part was when he, and so on. Finally we got in front of the building where the girls lived. This was on 4th Street and Avenue D in the projects.

Before the girls went up we started goofing on one part of the movie that seemed very funny. It was about 10:30 at night, and all of a sudden here comes two cops, so we kept quiet and moved back to the wall.

I was the smallest one there, and near the end of the line. There I was standing thinking he wasn't coming this way. But sure enough, he passes everybody and comes to me. He grabbed me by my neck and said get in the building, so as he opens the door to the building he kicks me in and shuts the door. He tells the other cop to stay by the window.

When the other cop signaled everything was alright he smacked me in the face, took his stick and rammed it across my leg, and I was yelling, "What the fuck are you hitting me for?" No answer. Then again, slam slam, slam, from one side of my face to another. Then a man started to walk out of the building.

Cop: Go on, yell police brutality, go on.

Paul: I'm not going to say anything. Anyway why should I, so you could beat the shit out of me some more?

As soon as the man left, BANG, he smashed my head against the wall.

Cop: Do you know what you did now?

Paul: All I know is that we were talking about a movie.

Then one of the girls ran over to the window and said in a surprised voice, "He's not even crying!" I grinned and said to myself, "I bet this not crying is making him hit me."

Cop: Get that girl!

Just then I smelled it, he was drunk. "Oh shit!" I said to myself.

Other cop: I couldn't get her. She cut out.

Cop: Let's bring him in the station.

At this time I wished there was another cop on duty in the station, but there wasn't. We get in the office.

Cop: Sit down, stand up, sit down, stand up.

Paul: What's a matter with you?

Cop: When I tell you to do something, you do it, you dig.

Paul: When are you going to let me go?

Cop: You address me as sir, yes sir, and no sir.

Paul: What kind of game are you playing man, why don't you let me go?

Cop: Shut the fuck up, and how much money do you have?

Paul: Just some change.

Cop: Let me have it.

As I went in my pocket I said, "Here's all I have." Then I dropped it on the floor.

Cop: Are you some kind of wise guy?

As the cop bent down to pick it up, one of my friends opened the door to peek in and I ran out of there as fast as I could.

My friend: You scared the shit out of me, you know that.

Paul: Thanks a lot. You opened that door just in time.

Since that day I never went back around that block, and I never said anything, because I know you can't beat a cop. Especially, if there isn't any adults around.

Overnight in Central Park

When I used to stay on 4th Street these girls and guys used to plan trips for the weekend and they invited me. They decided to go to Central Park and stay over one night. There was this girl there that always was looking at me, I think she liked me. Anyway, we got introduced.

We got there and it was a lot of fun. But then came night, no cops around, no one in sight. I couldn't sleep and this girl was awake too.

Paul: Hey, get some sleep.

Girl: I can't.

Paul: Go on, try.

Girl: Hey Paul, let's go for a walk.

Paul: Alright, but we can't go too far, we don't want to get lost.

Girl: But I do.

Paul: Alright, come on.

We started walking, then she started running. She ran into this bush by the lake and laid down.

Girl: Come on Paul.

I gently laid down beside her.

Girl: Oh, shit, they're calling us, cut out.

Paul: Come on, jump in the boat. Be quiet. They didn't see us.

She was lying down on her back, and said—

Girl: Paul, you're so smart, I really like you.

Paul: Stay there, don't move, and stop talking.

I laid on top of her and started making out with her. She lifted up her dress and put her hand on my . . . . She opened my. . . . Just then— "Hey, get out of that boat." The guard was calling.

I rowed the boat to the other side and grabbed her hand and ran, ran, ran until we got back to the others. The others were sleeping and I gave up and she gave up and we both fell asleep.

The next morning nobody said anything, because we acted like we didn't even know each other.

Social work and
other illness

None of my best friends are social workers.

I've thought a lot about this and the more I've thought the more I realize that this is the one single prejudice I have that is completely rational. I don't make any generalizations about social workers I haven't met. I've met a load of them, from all parts of the country, in all kinds of positions, all races, sizes, backgrounds, both male, female and none of these, and they have one important thing in common. I don't like them. I haven't liked them since I met my first one, long before I met street kids. The second, fourth, and seventy-fifth only added to my dislike. I'm still looking for the exception that supposedly proves the rule, but as I get older the chances look pretty slim.

Social work, to paraphrase, someone else talking about something else, is precisely the disease it professes to cure. Social workers are the carriers of that disease. It is a disease characterized by a tone of voice, a detachment, fright, and a particular kind of asexuality; all of which communicates an attempt at superiority over those they are ostensibly helping. . . . I believe social workers call these people "clients." I think I should make it clear at this point that I am talking about *trained* social workers, the kind with degrees, MSW's or others, and not the kind that are taken as they are from their communities as a few enlightened groups are doing today. (But I worry even about those few if the social workers get them in their clutches for "training.") I think this is an important distinction, since I believe most of the social workers' problems come from their education.

Now you know my prejudice. So what? What do I complain about and what have my complaints to do with the lives of street kids? I'm glad you asked.

Social work as a profession has grown over the years into a position of considerable power. It controls almost as much money as the educators and has an even firmer grip on the lives of the people who are supposed to benefit from the money it controls. It has reached this position of control and power not out of its successes or even its promises. It has developed into a system accountable mainly to itself out of a much more insidious process. By default.

Garbage collectors, sanitation men, sewage disposers, usually end up getting their demands from the public, sooner or later. The same with plumbers and other necessaries in the world of services. The reason is simple: no one else wants to do their work. Even the National Guard wouldn't go on for long collecting the garbage. We make special allowances for people who are doing the jobs we don't want to do or to think about. People bitch at mortician fees, but not seriously or for long because they really can't do without them. And here is where the parallel with social work stops. All the noble professions I have mentioned have a clear function. We leave them pretty much alone to do their job in their own way under pretty much their own terms. But, we know what it is they do.

Social work, on the other hand, gets the same kind of latitude, but its function is not at all clear. In an ugly kind of way, they propagandize all of us into believing that *they* are handling our garbage too, and that they really know what they're about and that they should be left alone to do our dirty work. They convince politicians, lawmakers, and policy makers that they are God's Garbage Men. That they have received the Word and are the keepers of The Truth. And people for hundreds of years, guilty about "the poor and unfortunate" and fearful of meeting the fate of Marie Antoinette, have turned over their conscience proxies to the "do-gooders" and rested easy that the world of the underprivileged is in good hands.

At first, the good-hands people were the mothers and daughters of the rich, acting out their *noblesse oblige* with the human sensitivity so long associated with royalty. Christmas baskets for the poor, second-hand clothes, and other remnants left to convince the *leavers* that the world was good, and they were better. As the poor grew in number, the proxies became more diffuse. Universities began training women to take the place of Lady Bountiful and to do so within a new professional definition called Social Work. The effect of this inclusion of yet another "helping" profession was to give easy entrance into the professional world. The requirements for completion of a social work degree were much easier, and still are, than requirements for the other "helping" professions of medicine, psychiatry, psychology, and nursing. So a lot of people, women mainly, crept into the back door of professionalism through the route of social work.

This could give rise to another important question. What would make someone *want* this quick and easy route to the intervention into the lives of the poor and the oppressed? What kind of people are these who look to the university to license their presumptuous judgments about people for whom they have so little empathy? People for whom empathy is degraded as inhibiting "professional distance" whatever that is.

Later men joined the profession and to a large degree took over its administration and control. For the most part these were men who couldn't make it into other professions, but were sensitive enough to see the potential gold mine in a field that had such blind, unquestioning donors. Social work public relations began inflating the social work balloon: Social workers were the dedicated people put here by The Lord to do his nonclerical labors. With the help of government, who always is in the market for Holy Men and big city fund raisers, who always have their eyes open for a fast buck, social work reached its present state of eminence. Today, United Fund campaigns and other "we gave at the office" deduction plans take in millions of dollars for "do-good" causes. Very few people know how little actually gets out of the hands of the "do-gooders" and into the hands of the communities of the poor.

Social work has become a pseudopsychiatric boondoggle supporting a lot of people who have no business in the lives of other people. It represents, more than any other single force in America today, a collection of Naked Emperors. People who have so clouded our eyes with their words and their incantations, that most people are too intimidated (and guilty) to confront them in their nakedness. Except for a few great people (far fewer than most other professions boast), people like Jane Addams and Jacob Riis, social work has the distinct honor of having produced the greatest number of drones of any university production line. They have produced, in a society that reveres production and productivity, less than any other profession. And they have been rewarded for their incompetence, year after year, with increased budgets, increased salaries, and increased autonomy. It's like giving airline pilots bonuses for plane crashes.

Social workers run the welfare system in America and have, through the years, helped to shape its policy. It is finally coming to light that this welfare system has been destroying and disabling those it has purported to help. And now that we know this, now that we know the system that has cost us all so much in lives and in money is such a dismal failure, we will close our eyes again and give the social workers another round.

I'm just getting to understand "Middle America." After being so media blinded for so long about the uncaring people of the Agnew generation, I realize that I've been had. Along with a lot of you. People have been paying, month after month, year after year, administration after administration, they have been paying the social workers' bills, signing their blank checks. They have bitched a lot about it, but in the way people always bitch about death, taxes, and the draft. But in their hearts they felt they were paying their proxies to do "God's work." Maybe they felt too superior for that, or bought their way off too cheaply, but they paid when they had a lot of more personal things to do with their money.

Finally, the poverty program. The ultimate social work-public relations conspiracy. Billions of tax dollars and billions of lines of newspaper space. The greatest show on earth. Promises for money. Money for promises. Headlines. Appropriations. Slogans. Pentagonisms. The War on Poverty. Mobilization for Youth. The Job Corps. Brigades. Platoons. Bugles. The social work swan song. An orgasm of spending and promising and swindling until one day . . . one day somebody out there in Americaland said it. Right out loud. "The emperor is naked." And other folks, with similar histories of deductions from their pay checks that went to nothing, said it too. The spending was over. A silent majority emerged with a little help from their friends, and they held up their hands and said "enough." And they gave us Richard Nixon as a sign of their fed-upedness. Not of their racism or their hatred of the poor, as our liberal spokesmen might have you believe, but out of the self-protective motive of wanting their money to buy something that works. I think even some of them wanted gratitude, which is not very godlike, but a little understandable given the media hard sell they were given.

As much as I disagree personally with Pentagon spending, I understand that people can be conned into accepting it longer than they will accept paying for social work lies. They know what tanks and bombs are and they have an idea of what they do. They also believe they work. As evil as it may be, they are paying for *something*. Hardware.

The social workers had an obligation to the poor and oppressed of the present and the future to show that money spent on people could also be paying for something. Instead they took the money and ran. And people have a right to be mad as hell. The net result of the social work hustle, of course, was to add to the job of polarizing the country. The poor are enraged about having so many promises, accepted in good faith, unkept and in many cases enraged about being worse off than ever.

The working man, scared as hell by press reports of the coming revolution, looks at his old pay checks and says, "What the hell have I been paying for?" And the social worker, still unscathed by his self-serving destructiveness, plans new ways to increase his cut without blowing his game.

Enter the social worker and the street kid.

As much as they don't like it, and only until they can work their way up to Administration, social workers are forced to be "where the action is." They are forced to be where it is, but not to be part of it. This was most obvious when the Poverty War was declared on the Lower East Side.

Storefronts opened and were immediately insured against having the "clients" or "target populations" (social work words) they were funded to help just by nature of the look, the style, the *ambiance* of the places they created. Green-walled storefronts, institutional green, with green half partitions and desks. "Come right in kids and make yourselves at home in our up-tight cubicles," they seemed to be saying. And sure enough, the kids didn't come in, right on schedule.

But like vampires cringe and run from The Cross, social workers are brought to their knees by other symbols. Statistics. You gotta have some kids in order to keep getting the bread. Enter relevance.

What street kids need next to love and attention is money. And since social workers are not programmed to give the former, they choose to use money as bait. As relevance. They started work programs. The World of Work, Mobilization for Youth called it, as if it were a kingdom from Disneyland. In The World of Work kids were paid between $30 and $40 a week to learn building skills. They were also to experience the gratification of achievement, building something with their own hands, getting the feel of what it means to be a *man*, to accomplish something. To be a part of creating rather than destroying.

So, at the beginning of a day in The World of Work kids would build a wall in the building bought for that purpose by the program. And after it was built, they would tear it down. And they would build it again. The World of Work.

Meanwhile, the building trades unions weren't taking young black or Puerto Rican kids into their apprenticeship programs in any numbers and most of the kids found themselves in a dead end. Set up for the big fall. Of course, the "agency" (social workers like to call their places "agencies," but it would be too much for them to call themselves "agents") was there with their Job Counselors if the kids decided on some other job, like pushing a garment rack up Seventh Avenue. Most kids knew about that route before the Job Counselor, so they kept their $30- or $40-a-week nothing training job as long as it lasted and then went back to the streets to look for some other hustle. In the meantime they had contributed to the agency statistics.

In other areas social workers showed similar insight.

A coffee house was opened and two rival gangs brought together to help renovate it. One side pulled a gun and the social worker in charge was fired on the spot. Lesson one.

After the jurisdictional battle was settled and the coffee house opened. the social workers insisted the kids sign a guest list when they entered, "so we'll know just who our customers are," they said. Street kids have a natural aversion to giving out this kind of information, since it's always used against them in one way or another. They were promised the guest list would be kept confidential. And since the whole coffee house thing was new and better than hanging out on the street corner, the kids gave in. When the first rumble broke out in the coffee house and the police were called, the first official act of the social workers in charge was to give the guest list to the cops. Lesson two.

In order to help settle a gang dispute that was to be resolved violently, a social worker set up a summit conference of the gangs involved. It was set up on the social worker's day off without his remembering that and when the day came the groups came together and he wasn't there. Both sides thought it was a trap and they fought. One kid was killed, thirteen badly hurt, sixteen arrested. Lesson three.

Three introductory lessons pointing out the clumsiness, dishonesty, and lack of sensibility that has characterized social workers' attempts in the world of street kids. Of course, anyone could have made those mistakes. And, of course, others have. It's a chaotic life, the life of the streets, and a hard one to try to figure or outguess. Only for social workers the mistakes are consistent, the dumbness seemingly a part of their approach to life, the dishonesty too predictable.

Social workers smile too damn much when there isn't anything to smile about. They smile when they're kicked and nobody buys such saintliness. They also smile as they pull the switch after they've gotten someone else to strap you in. They are emotionally dishonest because the most basic of their feelings—that of contempt for the people they "serve"—must always be masked. If they stop smiling for a minute, or if they respond honestly with love or with hate, they risk being left naked. Themselves. A regular old person without that professional distance. Most of them that I've met don't much like themselves. Especially naked.

Anyway there shouldn't be a profession called Social Work. It's too ill-defined and too patronizing and paternalistic in its connotation. There should be advocates, ombudsmen, counselors, therapists, huggers, helpers, players, and interpreters. There should not be checkers, hander-outers, judgers or better-than-youers walking around with such sweeping powers without being properly labeled for everyone's protection. Even policemen have to wear badges. There shouldn't be meddlers walking around at all.

For street kids, social work means a nine to fiver. A game player. Someone to be conned. Someone you have to lie to in order to get what you should get without having to lie. Someone who has the power to give you just enough to suffer in silence. Someone who says if you smoke pot you'll get hooked. Someone you just have to tolerate like the landlord, the teacher, and the cop. Someone you should cultivate like the drug dealer, the runner, or the pimp. Someone who knows The Man.

Street kids have known that the medium is the message long before McLuhan told the rest of the world. They never listen first to what someone says, but they search the cues for who he is. If what he says is consistent with that, he's okay. Even if you don't agree with the package. A rat who says he's a rat and acts like a rat has a place. But street kids are most sensitive to the honesty and consistency of "the message."

There's a big community meeting and I'm there with some kids. It's an emergency meeting on housing conditions and the guy who's running the meeting is a local social worker. I met him before and he told me he studied C. O. in social work school. I thought, "That's cool, they have a special course in Consciencious Objectors." But it turned out it was Community Organization.

One of the kids taps me on the shoulder.

"That guy. The guy in the front talkin'." Luis is pointing with his chin at the social worker meeting runner. "Does he make any bread doin' that shit?"

"Yeah," I tell him, "he does okay. I'd guess he makes about ten or twelve thousand."

"So how come he wears clothes that don't fit?"

I'm about to go into a whole thing about how some people don't think the way he does about clothes or how they look. That just because all of the kids on the street really dig clothes and look up to adults who've made it because they can really dig clothes, that shouldn't make them put down someone who digs other things. You know the rap. Straight tolerant libertarian.

I caught myself. This guy wore clothes that didn't fit as his slum uniform. Each rip in his pants was a battle star. Each wrinkle in his seersucker jacket was a service stripe.

He was trying to tell us he was poor.

"I guess he wants us to think he's poor," I answered, and Luis said, "The medium is the message," only he said it some other way.

Felix

Felix was locked up when he was twelve mostly because he was in his mother's way. The man she was living with didn't like Felix much and the feeling was mutual. There was a lot of tension. So Felix didn't go to school and his mother had a good case when she finally decided to get him out of the way. The court willingly prosecuted Felix for truancy (according to his school) and being unmanageable (according to his mother) and never listened to the other side of the story (according to Felix).

The court sent him to Youth House, New York City's destruction center for children from seven to sixteen (now called "Spofford Juvenile Center" to escape its infamy) and before he was there a week, he had been propositioned by a member of the staff, beaten by some older boys for "squealing" on that staff member, called a troublemaker by the social worker he reported to, and forced to change his name from Felix to "Ray Charles" because he had to wear tinted glasses. His troubles at Youth House didn't last long that trip. His lack of conformity branded him crazy, his unwillingness to involve himself with a homosexual cook after he was promised more and better food made him a downright traitor. So they shipped Felix to Bellevue for "observation." There's more than one way to get a twelve-year-old Puerto Rican to shape up.

But Felix didn't shape up. He was tough. He was at war. It was a war to make the world safe for being Felix and, suffer though he did for his patriotism to himself, he would not give in.

At Bellevue they didn't have any room in the children's psycho unit, so they locked Felix up with the violent adults. He was one of a few not in strait jackets or put in padded rooms. He ate with the derelict patients, most with their minds blown on rotgut or other exotic Bowery libations.

Once, the guy next to him at dinner spit in Felix's food, and Felix told the guard. The guard beat the guy with his club and locked him up, so Felix never told the guards anything after that. His observation period was coming to an end, he had ignored the questions of the psychologists probing his sex life and fooled around with the ink blots just enough to convince everyone he was at least as sane as the people showing them to him.

He was back in Youth House again and the next year on pretty much the same kind of intangible charge. He just didn't fit in to something or other.

This time he was used as a pawn in the perverted sexual games of two of the Youth House "supervisors." The staff had found a young homosexual boy and had brought two older boys, Felix one of them, into a room to force them into sexual action while the supervisors looked òn. The other boy refused first and he was beaten until he submitted. Felix refused and held out. He was sent back to his dormitory bloodied and with his glasses broken.

Later, he said of the Youth House supervisors, "They like to see you go through it. Then they laugh and make fun of you in front of everyone. It's how they get their kicks."

For speaking to a girl in the lunch room he was pushed down a flight of stairs. When he asked to speak to a social worker they laughed.

Felix was in Youth House for truancy. For skipping school regularly since the sixth grade. And for rehabilitation for this lack of educational motivation he was forced to continue his truancy, this time with official sanction, since the Youth House school was overcrowded and he wasn't allowed to attend. He didn't miss much. The best the school had then to offer was a record player, a TV, and some comic books. Or else you could sit quietly and watch your teacher silently reading *The New York Times*.

At no time during his various institutionalizations did he receive anything that might be called "therapy." At no time did anyone ask him how come he was missing school or what was bugging him. At no time was Felix anything more than another spic kid waiting to be old enough to make adult courts and adult prisons. But Felix fooled them. He was serious about his war to be himself. His war to be somebody better than all he was told.

He never went to school after the seventh grade. At fourteen he ran away with Pat, a part gypsy girl of twelve, and her parents had the cops out looking for them. They found them and sent them both to Youth House. Out again, the two took up living together again, were locked up again, took up again, living in this empty apartment and that, until finally, in desperation, both parents stopped having the kids locked up and just abandoned them to each other. They hustled from friends and relatives to stay alive, always living with the threat that at any time their freedom could be taken away, without notice.

When Felix was sixteen, he was working and getting tutoring with us at LEAP. Pat worked too and learned to read at the LEAP School. Their big thing was they wanted to get married. After all, after living together during the years when some kids are still watching Captain Kangaroo, one could hardly object on moral grounds.

Both Felix's mother and Pat's parents objected. Neither had ever provided even the most basic care or attention to the two kids when they lived at home, but they refused to let the kids live away from the threat of the cops. But the two of them managed to live pretty well anyway, setting up housekeeping and talking about problems and the future, making plans and loving each other with greater facility than most much older, legally laced couples. But they were not to be given their freedom. Under New York law, while a parent isn't often held responsible for the physical or emotional destruction or abandonment of a child, he is given full legal powers to punish or restrict a child. And punish and restrict they did.

When Pat finally became pregnant, she was fifteen. Felix was seventeen. The two of them had completed

the equivalent of four years of reading and other schooling in less than half that time, working and studying
with people they liked and who cared for them. Everyone thought that Pat's pregnancy would change her
parents' minds and they would allow them to be married,
but it didn't.

The only thing either family did was to visit Felix
and Pat's apartment whenever they chose, and take what
they had. Sometimes they didn't even bother to ask.
They took Pat's clothes, appliances that Felix saved for
or friends had given them, money when they could find
it and all the time, their privacy. Felix and Pat, by
surviving, had become the focus for family hustlers.
Their strength and survival made them prime targets,
just as it had all their lives, and just as it does for
anyone who breaks out.

But Felix persisted in his war. Surviving his battle
with the school authorities, the bombardment of his
Youth House experiences, his running skirmishes with
his mother, the guerilla warfare necessary to exist with
his chosen comrade in arms, surviving even the loss of
his childhood, Felix kept moving on, away from the
death that he believed was waiting if he surrendered.

He had gone as far as he was going to go with his
preparation for education. LEAP had taken him as far
as it could. Now Felix wanted college. He had never set
foot in an accredited high school, had spent only a
matter of weeks in junior high, but he felt he was ready
for college. Given his set of experiences it might have
been a surprise to find out what he wanted to study for.
He wanted to be a psychologist. He wanted to help kids
like himself. He would always understand kids' war
games.

A New England college agreed to take Felix on a trial basis if someone could pick up his tuition. It was an experiment, they said, one that they felt was important. Could a kid with high motivation and no formal credentials coming from a big city slum make it in a college far from the city and where the other students had more accumulated information? They were willing to try, and Felix was willing to try, and Pat was willing to try, and LEAP, as usual, found a way to underwrite it.

Pat had her baby, my godson Mark, and the three of them set off to the North country to college. Felix, the troublemaker, the truant, the nut, the nonconformist; Pat, the neglected kid who didn't even know a year before how her own body made babies; and Mark, who didn't know he was now a college brat. To college.

There were tough times. Felix had to learn the language of the middle class. He learned it fast but it was tough. Pat found herself with girls who talked and read and did things and she was forced to move out from behind the suffering passivity role of the ghetto wife. And they missed the city. As crazy as it sounds, for all the city had done to them, for all its bad memories and hard times, it was what they knew and they missed it. So Felix scraped some money together and bought a car from a guy who had to wait a while for the last payment and they visited the city whenever they could.

Then for a while they split up. Felix living at school and Pat in the city. As for Felix, he wanted some time to be the irresponsible college kid, like most everyone around him. For Pat it was a time of finding out who she was on her own. But through all of this, they both cared for Mark. They wouldn't put their own scars on their kid.

Felix finished his second year of college, got his Associate degree, right on schedule. His lack of credentials hadn't cost him any time once he got the knack of the college game. I saw him just before his graduation.

"I'm gonna take a year off from school, work a year or so and get my family thing together," he told me, "then maybe I'll go on and finish or not. I got a lotta things I can do for my people, and maybe I don't need no more school to do them."

Felix's war. Who could ever believe that the mother of his baby was still legally truant from school?

All I want

I'm learning more and more as time goes by. Sometimes I like what I learn. Sometimes I hate what I learn. Today I learned that white is white and black is black, and color and races mean something. No matter how bad whites want to help us, they always have something behind what they say and in what they do for us. I know that we are not handicapped and I know I'm not, so the only reason the whites help us is because they want to feel that they did something for the poor and handicapped, but instead of helping us they get something out of it.

I feel, and I want everyone to know, and especially the whites who are keeping us down, that I don't want power. All I want is to be heard as a person, *a human being,* because I was born the same way as the President and rich people, except that he fell in a clean bed and I fell in one that was a little dirty. But I tell you one thing, that I didn't come out of my mother's ass so don't treat me like shit.

El Barrio

I was born in El Barrio of New York. I was brought up a funny way but I'm glad I was. From the first moment I was born my mother never caged me in. I learned everything about the streets while growing up. When I was about 7 I got my first fuck. It was a small peanut but the girl didn't mind. I learned the good and the bad—not from my mother but from all my mothers, brothers and sisters in El Barrio. I seen shoot outs with blacks and cops and gangs killing each other. Bullets going through my window. I learned everything I had to learn to survive in the streets from running when it was time to protect your pride and how to handle manipulators. I remember this one guy: his mother kept him in a cage all the time since he was a baby. That went on for years and years. Then it came. It was time to set the poor boy free, but it was too late. The dope was rising and there was rioting all over. When the guy got to the streets of El

Barrio he didn't know one thing about street life, so every time the survivors of the streets got a hold of him they took his money, they beat him up, they manipulated him like crazy until the guy got hip to himself and started fighting back. He started doing everything the junkies were doing like robbing, taking dope to make him look big—but it didn't last long. The poor guy died of an overdose of dope. The guy's mother yelling and screaming, "My son! My poor boy!"—but she didn't know it was her fault. But I was alive, and kept learning everything I could about this ugly world I lived in.

I started learning about this white who supposedly discovered this country, and how much they try to keep us in a pot with the lid on, until one day they didn't put the lid on tight and everyone in the pot who was tired of being suffocated in the pot started boiling until it boiled so much that the lid flew open and we were free. But we were in the same position that guy was when his mother set him free. Some of us dying trying to be heard and stay free, trying to do it peacefully until we were shot in the back or hung for looking at a white broad. And now we know we've got to fight fire with fire.

Education

I

Marching out of cookie-cutter colleges
Come the gingerbread teachers
Covered with the paper armor of degrees, licenses and
    contracts
they come to be tempered in the heat
    of ghetto schools
It will be trial by fire.
Most of them will get badly burned and will go
    away.
Others stay, each burn serving as callous
against the next
working only to survive
knowing that survival is easier here since
    no one
expects too much.
Still others stay for revenge
to inflict scars of their own for their own reasons.

The gingerbread teachers with all their papers
Will pass through the poor kids' schools.
No one ever told them it would be
like this.
The kids come too
First day fresh come the little ones looking
wide-eyed and forward
to school
looking forward to being Big.
They come
innocent
hopeful and typically child
in their trust.
The older kids come
but their eyes are different.
They are knowing and cynical.
They have the secret of things to come
but they never let on
to their trusting little brothers
almost like they know
how nice it is
not to know.
But they will play the game
(only for the first few
back-from-the-monotony-of-summer days) and
then they will stop with the annual fall masquerade
and get down to the old routine.
Sniffing glue in the school basement
hookey
empty apartments and gigs with the girls
hiding from the attendance officer and the cops and
their moms.
Little brother will have to learn his reality

for himself.
And little brother does.
Midway through P.S. whatever
in the fifth grade or the sixth
he will suddenly die
his kid trust destroyed along with any vestige
of self-respect.
The school will keep his body in attendance to collect
their daily ransom from the state.
It will take five or six years of concussion
for this trusting little kid to finally say
"these people don't give a damn
    about me
these people are teaching me a lotta shit."
But it will happen. The Compulsory Education Law
makes it compulsory.

II

Everyday
lesson plans from headquarters are unfolded by the
                teachers
who like field marshals of futility
unfold their maps and plans of battle
from their distant sources.
And as field commanders are prone
to "take the hill at any cost"
the teachers run their preprogrammed curricula
with a similar disregard for the lives
of real people.
Everyday
kids actually sit down and write the word
AIM
if they can write

at the top of the page
AIM
right out of the curriculum guide
for the teachers.
You know.
The part that explains to the teacher
the AIM of this particular section of The Plan
in the Overall Scheme.
And the teachers
not even investing enough of themselves to remove
the labels from their prepacked pills—
from their rigid adherence
to the guide book
mindlessly write AIM
on the blackboard and ask the kids to copy
their teachers college instructions.
Like the Pledge of Allegiance to the Flag
    that came first in the morning
this ritual is meaningless since no one understands
    the words.
Like having to wear white shirts and ties to school
    to show proper respect to something
or other
even though your clothes are few
and your mother's burdens many
Like hygiene classes rapping on proper diet and venti-
                lation
    when you have control of neither.
Like a guidance counselor who never gave guidance
or counsel
telling you to quit school and get a job
And then those lying posters on the subway walls saying
"stay in school."

"Success" in this place means accepting
   the pointless and the crazy
playing as if the world right outside
wasn't there
becoming less of whatever bright color you are
in favor of a uniform shade
of grey.
AIM: To make *Them* like *Us*
METHOD: Neutralize curiosity and spontaneity
   demolish spirit by constant reminders of
inadequacy
ignorance
and weakness.
SUMMARY: A free and happy kid is a demanding kid
and only unions can make demands.

III

Some people say that kids and teachers
   in poor kids' schools
are both victims
and the people who say this
are usually teachers
and they say it when someone asks
"Whatever happened to that wide-eyed little kid?
How come he dropped out of life
when he started out so well?"
And the Educators
verbally connected to the victimized
(but who really know what power is
like few others in our world)
get a grant from the government
and do a Study.

"Whatever Happened To The Wide-Eyed Kid": is called
                    something else
that fits into the guidelines
and costs a thousand times more than the reason
    it had to be written
a thousand times more on the post mortem
than on the living kid.
There will be findings
talk about environment
deprivation
and motivation
and after the appropriate Sigmas and Standard
    Deviations
it will conclude (in effect):
WHAT WE GOT HERE
IS THIS BUNCH OF SCREWED UP KIDS
WHO DON'T GIVE A *DAMN*
FOR LEARNING
AND WE TRIED
OH, HOW WE TRIED
BUT YOU KNOW HOW IT IS
Only they will say it orchestrated in 579 pages ending up
    with recommendations
leading to the support of someone's pet
remedial programs.
Remedial.
Remedial money flows from the government
under various titles
of various acts of congress
With a typical disregard for simple logic
it forces kids into afterschool programs
with the same failing processes
and people

that lost them in the first place.
The kid
it turns out
sees Remedial as Punishment
while the teacher sees it as time and a half.

IV

Education we are told
is big business
and that is misleading.
It is *a* big business
but not like
Big Business.
It is a big business because so much money is
    made from it
but it is now *like* Big Business because it is not account-
                able
for a successful product
and the stockholders never get
an honestly audited Annual Report.

V

Poor kids
with all their problems
are kids who are eager and anxious
to learn.
They have been forced by their world to learn fast
and learn well
but they have been cursed
with an eye for authenticity.
They know a swindle when they see one
and they have the audacity to laugh

at naked emperors.
They will not learn from Dick and Jane books
when they do not live in a Dick and Jane world.
They can't learn from teachers who care more
about late slips
than about them.
They can't believe anyone
who tells them they are equal
instead of teaching them
How.

Luis

*L*uis was born in 1947. On the day he was born, Robert F. Kennedy was already twenty-two. Nineteen years later Luis and Robert Kennedy met in a Lower East Side tenement at 623 East 12th Street. 623 East 12th Street was born in 1900. All of this is important.

I guess of all the kids I knew who first walked into LEAP in its early days, I was closest with Luis. I was only ten years older than him and even before he reached New York's legal drinking age of eighteen, we were drinking buddies. After some of the incredible days in LEAP, on the streets or in the courts, Luis and I would sit down in our living room at a round oak table and we would talk about the world. We nearly always killed the half a bottle of Irish whiskey that was left from the last discussion of the world held usually no more than a few days before.

"Well, we solved some more of the world's problems," we would say to Michelle as she came downstairs for something or other and saw us reaching the end of one of our philosophical duels, "Tomorrow night we'll finish the rest of them." But tomorrow night we found new unexplored territories. And we went on like that. Twice a week or so we would put on some Miles Davis or Nina Simone and kill a bottle. Neither of us ever got sick but we sure didn't make much sense. Except to each other. We always made some important points that the other always seemed to understand, even if no one else around did. Irish whiskey lets people communicate.

Just before Luis wandered into LEAP in 1964, he had been the War Lord of the Latin Crowns, a fairly good-sized gang that held a fairly good-sized chunk of territory during the late fifties and early sixties when gangs were running at full steam. Luis' function as War Lord was to mediate and if that failed to plan battle strategy. He had an army of nearly a thousand soldiers at his disposal, if the war was a racial one— several hundred if it was an intramural dispute. And he was the finest of behind-the-lines strategists.

But in 1966, with the racial tensions mounting, we began to edge apart. Luis was on the staff of LEAP, as were most of the other original LEAP kids, drawing a good salary as housing coordinator—organizing tenements and running rent strikes. Others were putting out a newspaper called *What's Happening* that was a brighter yellow than any of William Randolph Hearst's tabloids. But basically factual. Still others were involved in organizing street kids into a lobby or getting all the neighborhood groups together into a federation. But through all the activity and change, through all the successes and not-so-successes, Luis stood out as the brightest light. He was the leader. The one who knew how to rap. The guy who understood power.

So when the W.E.B. DuBois Club came along and gave him the "what are you doing being a reformer when your people need you?" rap Luis listened. They really wanted Luis. A proud, articulate, brilliant young Puerto Rican that they could use. The times said that Luis should go that route. But he waited because he was still involved in his organizing and he couldn't justify leaving his people to help his people.

On May 3, 1966, Senator Robert F. Kennedy visited LEAP and Luis took the Senator on a tour of the building he organized. The May 17, 1966 issue of *What's Happening* reported under a headline "Kennedy Visits East Side Slum" and a four-column picture of Luis pointing something out to the Senator. ". . . At the building (Luis) told Kennedy that the building was so dilapidated that once a tenant slammed a door and a whole wall came tumbling down. The tenants in the building have been withholding their rents for the last two months.

"Kennedy visited the second-floor apartment of Mrs. S. T. who lives with her five grandchildren in two small rooms. The Senator listened while Mrs. Talentino shouted her complaints in Spanish and (Angel) another LEAP member, interpreted.

"Mrs. T. told him there has been no light in the toilet for three years. She said that since the rent strike began the agent has been coming around every day asking for the rent. (The landlord is Jer-Ron Realty, 346 E. 149th St., The Bronx.)

" 'You tell the agent,' Senator Kennedy said, 'that I

told him to come see me at the Post Office building!'. . ."

The landlord never visited the Senator at the Post
Office building and soon after the Senator's LEAP
visit, Luis became convinced that no landlord would
ever take up such an invitation. He became convinced
that landlords didn't have to listen to anyone. That his
people were being killed by law-flaunting landlords.
And there was nothing he could do about it. At less
than half the pay he was making at LEAP he went to
the DuBois Club. We talked about it some and he just
said that the way things were he didn't think he had
any choice. I was an OK white guy, but there were a
lot of white guys around who weren't so OK and he had
to go and take care of business. I think he was right in
what he said. And what he wanted. He would have to
try *another* way.

623 East 12th Street just continued to deteriorate.
The Senator brushed off the pressures to be President.
The craziness that had surfaced with the sixties and
doubled with the death of Robert Kennedy's brother,
doubled and tripled again with explosions of violence
across the country. Luis moved into even more revolutionary action. The Senator accepted the challenge of
the Presidency, and 623 East 12th Street just hung
on.

I didn't see Luis very much. He was busy and so
was I, and our circles weren't the same. Kids told me
he was a member of this or that super secret group and
I listened, remembering the nights we solved the
world's problems. When we did meet, by chance, it was
unpleasant. He would be with his crowd and had to
score points. He'd say, "How's it goin' Whitey?," or

"Still tryin' t' save your people, uh?" And I'd just look at him and walk on.

The news of Robert Kennedy's death hit me hard. The pointlessness of it. He was the only man in politics I had any feeling for and he was dead. It didn't make any sense. But neither did it make any sense only a few months later when I got a call telling me that Luis was dead. He was shot trying to stop a hotel clerk from shooting his partners in an attempted robbery. To save his friends he pulled a toy gun and was killed instead.

Two months later the last tenant moved out of 623 East 12th Street. It's still standing. But it's condemned.

The dean and I

When I was in school the teacher had all the power, like the dean. One time I was cutting class and I got caught by a teacher. He said, "What are you doing in the hall?"

Ralph: I am going to the bathroom.

Teacher: Where is your pass?

Ralph: I left in a hurry, I forgot the pass.

Then he grabbed me and took me to the dean. When we got to the dean's office there was a guy hung up in front of the dean's office because he didn't have his tie on right, so he hung him up in front of his office. The guy was saying, "Let me down." I got scared because I thought he was going to do the same thing to me, and then the time came for me to go in. I was scared shitless. When I got in he said, "Why were you cutting class Mr. Romero?"

Ralph: The class is boring, I don't learn nothing.

Dean: I'm going to give you a chance, but next time you come here for cutting class I'll deal with you.

So I left, but still scared.

The next day I came to school and went to history class. So I was gaffing with a friend sitting next to me until class started, but when the teacher came in she caught us gaffing about something nasty, so—

Teacher: Where did you learn to speak like that!

Ralph: In the streets.

Teacher: You know you were baptized from a needle from a record player.

Ralph: Your mother!

Teacher: You nasty bastard! Step outside. Here is a referral card, report to the dean.

Ralph: No, you started it.

SLAP. She slapped me, I grabbed her hands.

Teacher: "Let me go you bastard." Then another teacher came by. "Would you mind taking this kid to the dean?"

The Accomplice: No not at all.

Ralph: You better let me go, if you don't you and me are going to . . .

The Accomplice: You try and I'll kick your butt.

Ralph: Try it!

He picked me up. I was kicking and fighting until we got to the dean's office. The dean wasn't there, so me and the accomplice started fighting and then the dean came in.

Dean: What's going on in here?

The Accomplice: We have a wild cat, he told a teacher off.

Dean: Alright, you can leave, I'll take care of it. He locked the door. I told you that if I saw you in here again that I was going to take care of you right.

Ralph: Yeah, but she started it.

Dean: No buts.

He took his watch off and put it on the table and threw his ring on the floor and then he started hitting me.

After the fight the dean suspended me until my mother came in. I was scared to tell my mother because I thought she might kick my ass. So every morning my mother sent me to school I stood out in the streets. I met this guy in a backyard one day and he was sniffing glue.

Ralph: How is that stuff?

Glue Sniffer: Not bad. You want to try it?

Ralph: Don't know, I never tried it before.

Glue Sniffer: It's not bad, it gives you a good head. It makes you feel like flying, and you see things like god and angels.

Ralph: Wow! Let me try it.

Glue Sniffer: Ten sniffs for ten cents.

Ralph: Alright.

But when I put the bag up to my nose the smell was so strong that it almost burned my nose off. But after ten sniffs I got use to it.

The day went fast that day, so when I got home my mother was waiting for me.

Mother: Why didn't you go to school?

Ralph: Yes I did mom.

Mother: You liar. Your brother went to your class and you weren't there.

SWOP.

Ralph: But mom, the dean suspended me from school and I was scared to tell you because I thought that you was going to kick my ass.

SWOP.

Mother: I told you about using that kind of language in the house, in the street yeah, but in the house no.

The next day me and my mother went to school to see the dean. When we got there the dean started telling my mother what a bad boy I was and my mother just stood there saying, "Yeah, yeah, yeah, yeah, that's right." Then he asked my mother for permission to spank me every time I got out of line, but what he really meant was that he was going to kick my ass. So my mother agreed with him because she thought he was saying the truth.

The next week I was in art class and the teacher wanted some errand boys so I volunteered.

Teacher: Ralphie, take this across the hall.

So I went across the hall. When I got there I knocked on the door, opened it and walked in and put it on the table and then walked out. All of a sudden he got mad and slammed the door and hit me in my back. I got mad and kicked the door and then I ran. After I took a couple of other things to some other class I started back to my art class. Before I got to the art class the bell rang. The teacher that hit me in the back with the door called me.

Teacher: Hey you, come over here a minute.

So I tried to run but I slipped and he grabbed me and pushed me against the wall.

Ralph: Let me go you motherfucker, if you don't you better not step out of this school.

But he didn't let me go so I started fighting with him. My tears were coming down. The hall was full of guys and girls I knew. I was embarrassed so I swang at him and he ducked and I hit another teacher in the

face. "Why'd you hit me, I didn't do anything to you."
"I'm sorry." Then all of a sudden the dean appeared.
My heart went straight to my ass. I knew I was cooked.
I remember what happened a couple of days ago and
the way he beat the shit out of me.

Dean: What the hell is going on here?

Teacher: This kid came into my class whistling and
took something from my table.

Ralph: You damn liar! My art teacher sent me on
an errand to take something to your class so I put it on
your desk and walked out and then you slammed the
door and hit me in the back so I kicked the door.

The dean took me into his office.

Dean: You know, you're a pain in the ass.

Ralph: It ain't my fault, he ain't got no right to
grab me and push me around.

Dean: Alright, go to lunch.

I went to the park and I came in late. I got a late
pass and went to my official class. When I got there my
teacher sent a couple of guys on errands. While we were
walking through the hallways my tie wasn't on right,
and then again the dean. He was getting to be a pain
in the ass to me. Everywhere I went there he was. He
stopped me.

Dean: "Time me to see how fast I can tie this tie."
He took my tie and made a knot and started choking
me. "Hey, three seconds, that's really great." He did the
same thing to the other guys too.

A couple of weeks after, we moved to the Bronx, I
was glad to get out of there, but it was no different uptown. Over there I stood in the same math class for
three years, in the same grade, 9th. Now I wish I could
go back and give that dean a piece of knowledge.

"*Your best friend is your enemy*"

One day I met a group of guys and they asked me if I wanted to join their club so I said, "Hey, why not!" I didn't know they were punks until later.

One day we were walking through this alley and then a group of guys started throwing bottles at us, so we started throwing bottles back until we ran out of bottles, and then everyone went home. The next day one of the guys who was throwing bottles at us came over to us, "You guys hit one of our boys in the head yesterday."

"Well, you guys started throwing the bottles at us, so we threw them back."

"Well, you guys better get ready, because I'm going to get my gang."

"If that's the way you want it."

"Tomorrow at 5:00, on Fourth Street."

"Okay!"

So we went to our club and played it cool for the next day.

"Alright, how many guys have knives?"

"I do."

"I do."

"I do."

"Okay, bring them to the club tomorrow."

"Alright, let's forget about it until tomorrow. Let's get some girls."

"Put on some records."

"Go buy some bottles of wine."

We got stoned.

The next day we were ready for the fight. At 5:00, when it came around to fight, we got together and started walking up Fourth Street. I was in front of the guys with my brother. When we got half way up the block me and my brother looked around to look at our boys, but they all cut out. We tried our best to keep it cool. When we got face to face with the other gang we started talking about the guy who got hit on the head, and then the guy who started the whole thing got into a fight with my brother. My brother was doing good, he fucked him up.

"Who do you want to fight."

"I don't know."

So the president of the other gang said, "Hey, Ray, you fight him."

"Alright."

As I started taking off my shirt the guy jumped me and started hitting me.

"You dirty motherfucker, you sniked him."

So my brother grabbed him and felt like kicking his ass, but he let it go by. There were about 40 of them.

We couldn't fight all of them, so the big fight was on. The biggest guy from the other gang wanted to fight my brother.

"You can't fight him."

"Don't worry, I'll do my best."

Then when they were getting ready to fight, a guy who didn't like what was going on said, "So choose to fight the guy."

The guy who was on our side fucked the other guy up. The guy was bleeding from his eye. After that everyone left.

"Thanks a lot."

"Anytime you need my help, let me know."

After that me and my brother went home. We were so mad. We started looking for our so-called friends, but we could never find them. If we had found them we were going to kick their asses. We got tired of looking for them, so we started looking for new friends, and so me and my brother split up. He went looking for guys his age, I did the same thing. We found friends, but we didn't know that the friends I found and the friends he found were the same gang, but I was with the young guys and my brother was with the older guys. My brother is a mean motherfucker and became Pres of the gang and made me Pres of the young guys.

One day we got into an argument with this guy so he went and got his boys, but I didn't know it was the same gang I was in before that cut out on us, but with different guys.

I jumped up, "Tomorrow, at 5 o'clock, F.D.R. Drive." This time I was sure my boys weren't going to cut me loose.

That day we paid them back for what they did to me and my brother. I wish you were there to see them run and leave their Pres who I knocked out. One guy was making believe he got shot, "They shot me in the leg," running across the bridge. Everyone else just ran, me and my boys did too, cause the cops came. That day was a beautiful day for me.

Shoplifting

Me, my brother and some friends went to Orbach's. We went upstairs to the boys' department. There were two black dudes up there. They were trying to steal some knits. One of them took a couple of knits and put them in back of his pants. He and his friend started down the escalator, but they didn't know that there were two policewomen following them, so we tried to help them. We jumped in front of the police-women.

"Hey brother, run!"

They didn't pay any mind to us.

"Hey you stupid motherfucker, run! The cops!"

It was too late. The cops grabbed them and us.

"Let us go, we didn't do anything."

"That's what you think."

They took us into a room in the back. The black dude who had the two knits didn't know what to do.

"Take it out and throw it somewhere."

He took them and threw them on the floor. The cops started searching us but they didn't find anything, so they started looking around and found the two knits.

"Who do these belong to?"

"Not me."

"Not me."

"Not me."

"Alright, come with us."

They took us into this office. There were a couple of plain clothes cops. They started asking questions. They were trying to play it slick. They took me into this room.

"Did you take the knits?"

"No."

"Who did?"

"I don't know."

He kicked me in the leg.

"Who did it?"

"I don't know."

Kick.

"You still don't know?"

"I don't know."

"You want me to kick a little harder?"

"I don't know who took the knits."

He kept kicking me and I still said I didn't know, and then my brother went in and he started on him. My friend, he wasn't scared of the cops, but I was. The cop started pushing my friend around.

"I'm going to get my father to kick your ass."

"You don't say."

They took him to a little room in the back. I could hear him bouncing from one wall to another.

When my brother came out he said, "Shit, they're

kicking the shit out of Pepi. They might do the same to us."

"Don't worry, take it like a man. If they ask you for your name don't tell them."

They took the black dude in after my brother came out.

They stopped kicking Pepi's ass, they had him in there for around twenty minutes. They called me in.

"This boy says you took the shirts."

"He's a damn liar. We were trying to help you and now you say I took it." My tears were running down my face. "I'll tell you the truth now, this motherfucker took the knits. He's lying, ask the other two guys." The other two guys came in. "This man says I took the knits."

"He's lying, he took the knits."

The cop knew that my brother was one of these guys so he lined them up.

"Which one is your brother."

My brother was looking at me shaking his head telling me not to say anything. The cop caught my brother shaking his head and telling me no.

"Turn around and face the wall. Which one is your brother and what's his name?"

"I don't know."

"What do you mean you don't know."

"My mother never told me his name."

They started laughing, and the guys too. The cop let us go and kept the black dude in there. When we got to the hall of the store we ran out of that store and never went back.

Sniffing

After a month in the ghetto I didn't know anything about how to rob or smoke, until I met a guy. He was a nice guy but I didn't know that he smoked pot and sniffed glue until a week later.

"You want to try it?"

"I don't know, I never tried it before."

"It's good."

The glue bag was dry but my friend knew all about glue sniffing. He played with it a little while and made it soft. I took the bag and started sniffing it.

"I like it."

"Bet. Tomorrow let's buy a couple of tubes of glue."

I couldn't wait for the next day to come, I was thinking about it so much that the whole day went fast. When I saw my friend we went and got some tubes of glue. We went to the backyard. The yard was so dirty it looked like a garbage dump. He knew the yard like the palm of his hand.

"Come this way. Watch out for the nails."

"These people are lazy motherfuckers."

"What do you mean Ralphie?"

"Instead of bringing the garbage downstairs, they throw it out the window."

"Oh now I know what you mean."

He took me into a broken down building.

"Welcome to the time tunnel."

"Wow! This place is out of sight."

So we started putting the glue into a one pound bag. We started sniffing. I was having a hard time sniffing, but my friend he was sniffing like it was air. After a while I got used to it. I started seeing colors and felt like I was in another world. I liked it so much that I kept on doing it, until one day while I was sniffing my big brother and my little brother caught me and took me home.

"Mom, we caught Ralphie in the yard sniffing glue."

She took the bag and burned it on the stove. After that she took me and kicked the shit out of me. She punished me and she told my aunts. They all came down and lectured me, but I didn't pay any mind to them. Until one day, me and a group of girls and a couple of guys bought some tubes of glue. We decided not to go to the time tunnel, so we found a really small alley. We all squeezed in, I was all the way in the back with a girl. Me and the girl were having fun. We would sniff for a while and get a nice dream and then we would stop and I started rapping.

"Come on, let me get some."

"Some what?"

"You know."

"I don't know, tell me."

"Alright, I want some pussy."

"I ain't never going to give it up until I get married, then I'll give all my pussy to my husband."

"You know what's wrong with you?"

"What?"

"You still got that shit your mother told you when you started growing tits."

"No I don't."

"So why don't you let me get some?"

"There's too many people here."

"So let me feel you up."

"Alright."

But just when I was getting to enjoy it— "The cops!" I didn't hear the girl say the cops I was so busy enjoying it. All of a sudden there was a light in my face. Everyone threw their bags away. One of the girls tried to get away, but the cop tripped her, so everyone tried to get away. The cop started pushing us back into the alley.

"Hey Joe, hurry up, they're trying to get away."

The other cop came just in time to catch me.

"Where do you think you're going?"

"Nowhere."

He picked me up and threw me back into the alley. I had a stick of gum, I took it and started chewing it so the cop wouldn't smell the glue on my breath. After that

"Alright, let's start moving, and if any of you try to run I'll beat the shit out of you."

I believed him, but one of the girls didn't so she tried to get away. The cop grabbed her, she started kicking and hitting the cop. The cop carried her all the way to the street. The sergeant was out there. They started putting us into the police car, but when they got to the girl who was fighting with the cop.

"What's going on here?"

"This girl doesn't want to come peacefully."

"You ain't my father, let me go."

The sergeant grabbed her and threw her into the car. By the time we got to the police station the cop's hat was on the floor and his hair was all messed up. The cop started asking us where we lived and our age. I gave my right address but when it came to the age I told him I was 14. He asked me "What year?"

"1952."

"If you were born in '52 you'd be 17."

"Oh, I forgot, it was '55. Then you'd be 14. Right?"

"Right."

My little brother came in, "He's lying, he's 16."

I thought I was cooked, that when you were 16 you went to jail. They let us go because it was our first time. When I got out I kicked the shit out of my little brother and never sniffed glue again.

Drugs

Drugs are everywhere. Anyone can buy any kind of drug on almost any street, any day, any time. It's one of the few conveniences New York shoppers are offered. Chicken Delight and door-to-door dope.

Street kids see these drugs as part of the street smorgasbord. A sniff of this, a taste of that, a snort of the other, a shot of something else. The drugs of choice are pills (amphetamines, barbiturates, hypnotics, opiates, and hallucinogens), powders, (heroin and cocaine), and plants (marijuana, kief, and hashish). Most everybody smokes plants. The powder people get the most attention from the press and the courts. The pill takers are the craziest and make the most trouble. Then, of course, there are the indiscriminate ones who take whatever they can get, in whatever combinations come along. The winos of junkidom.

I think it was 1963 when I first tried to bring the

drug problem out of the streets and into the meeting rooms of the large fraternal and religious organizations. They made me feel like the weirdo author guest on the Johnny Carson Show—keeping me waiting through the whole damn boring meeting and then hurriedly, as an embarrassed afterthought just before adjournment, they would give me a few minutes to speak while most of the members were putting on their coats.

"Drugs are killing children," I would say, "fourteen- and fifteen-year-old kids are dying from overdoses while I sit and watch. We need help. We have to get together and find some way to stop this before more kids die." I ended, "Maybe if you don't help, it'll spread to your kids." And they smiled their damn patronizing smiles, the Elks and the Knights of Columbus and the American Legion, and told me, curtly, that they gave already. At the office. Each of them was supporting some kind of summer camp or other and what they didn't know about wouldn't hurt them.

All of a sudden these same guys, these pillars of the community, are experts on drugs. Now they're speaking in all the schools.

There are two groups of people who know about drugs: junkies and doctors. And most doctors only know how to prescribe them. If you have to pick some- one to lecture your kids or your school or your group about drugs, pick someone from Synanon or Daytop or the local residential addiction encounter programs. A kid who's grown up and off of drugs. Who's been through the lies and the pain of drugs. That's who knows. And that's who your kid will listen to, if he's going to listen to anyone. Police programs showing real needles and bent spoons and sugar cubes. Kids are always faced with know-nothing experts. Horror stories. Kids listen because they're a captive audience. They get out of school and light up a joint or sniff some glue and laugh at the day's entertainment.

It's a joke to talk about educating kids about the dangers of drugs when there is so much to be made from their sale and such motivation for their use. Cigarette advertising has compensated for the fact that cigarettes cause cancer and there isn't the profit in tobacco that there is in narcotics. With a 10,000 per cent profit from the fields to the needle, no education program in the world is going to change the dope picture by itself, and dope doesn't cause cancer. If you're looking to die, which a lot of street kids accept pretty openly, then you might as well die happy. That's the advertisement for dope. And kids are going to buy that message until we find a way to let them live happy.

While mostly everyone is looking into the evils of dope, few are looking squarely at the problem. Fewer are looking behind it. Why are kids taking drugs? Is it only because they're there?

For street kids, dope is adaptive. A way to cope by copping out. It's not simply some weird compulsion that drifts down on some weak character and lands him in hell. It's a considered, sometimes singular way out of the deadly circus of the streets.

Imagine being lost in a minefield, alone, with a map in one hand and a syringe full of dope in the other. Imagine seeing your buddies who have used the same map getting blown apart before your eyes, the lucky ones dying, the not so lucky lying around you missing some part or other, some few getting out and away. On the other hand, there are those in your dream who have taken the needle route. And you know that most of them didn't make it out either. So your decision isn't going to be too rational. Either you're going to have to believe you're a better map reader and a lucky son of a bitch or you're going to have to say you won't end up like the other guys who took the needle. But you're getting tired of standing still and you have to make the choice. What do you do?

I am in no way condoning the use of drugs. Merely explaining its prevalance. There are some pretty workable alternatives and people who can get some peace and objectivity can find these solutions. You can form a chain, learning from the mistakes (and maybe death) of others. You can clear an area and stay there, slowly expanding your territory into a larger and larger haven. But the motivation to drugs doesn't end by finding successful treatment techniques. Now kids have to go through the drug cycle and its lying, stealing, getting arrested, being sick and seeing death, before they can work their way out. There will have to be a huge effort made at preventing drug use and it isn't going to come out of the present horror story-punishment approach. It's going to come by offering kids more personal and satisfying ways out of their minefields. It will start by adults acknowledging the minefield's existence, waking up from the fogginess of old American Dreams, and risking some empathy with the perceptions and condemnations of our youth. There's nothing so crazy-making as someone telling you that your pain isn't real, that what you see before you is really something else.

Things will begin to improve when, once the common problem is acknowledged and the sleep-eye gone, the adults become part of the chain or part of the clearing party and stop being the ones pushing the kids to their death. Translated into action, that means adults are going to have to start listening to their kids instead of the professional condemners of kids and then they're going to have to join the revolution against corruption, hypocrisy, materialism, and violence. There's not much of a chance for that. So we're going to have a lot of dead kids.

It always hurts, when I look at the kids on the street using drugs, to know that the only adults they will find in their search for childhood are adults who won't let them have it. Teachers, social workers, policemen, judges, and jailers. That's the chain we give the kids and we wonder why they don't love us for our concern. Street kids or any kids can never forgive us for giving our proxies away to the enemy. Letting somebody else do the "caring." That's become our national pastime. Copping out. And isn't that what drugs are all about?

Police corruption

There's an old saying, that if you're going to steal,
Steal from the rich and not the poor.
I seen something that shook my pants down.
There's a candy store on 13th Street between B & C.
This little old man runs that store, and the store is kept
open on Sundays.
So the people can get their groceries for that day.
I was in there one Sunday after coming from a baseball
game
A cop comes in and the other stayed in the car.
The cop told the old man, "Hey, Bud,
You have a license to keep this store open on Sundays?"
The old man says,
"I have a license, yes."
Then, right away, he started talking to the old man a

whole bunch of bullshit, like:
"Your store isn't supposed to be open, you know.
You could get locked up.
Grocery stores can't be open after certain hours, BUT
I'll give you a break." The old man said, "Thank you, but
I didn't know that, I just was told by the people that I
should open on Sundays."
The cop: Never mind that!
I am telling you that you are not to be open.
Old man: Okay, then I close the store now.
The cop: You don't have to.
Listen,
Let me talk to you.
At that time the cop took him to the back of the store.
When the old man came out with the cop, the old man
seemed kind
of happy
And sad.
The old man went into the cash register and gave the
cop some
money,
and a case of beer. Then the cop left with what he had
stolen from the old man. The old man asked me, "What
do you
want?" "Nothing now, you made me wait so long." I
just said
that so that he wouldn't think I was listening to them.
I guess the old man thought the cop wouldn't come back
now,
but I knew
He'll be back.
After that Sunday, the same cop came back every
Sunday,

From Sunday to Sunday.
The old man finally realized he was being taken off.
Robbed.
Now this old man
Doesn't make a lot of business, because of the neigh-
borhood
he's in.
It's a Dead End block,
There's a lot of garages there,
And a little bit of people. All the people on the block
the adults and kids
Have and almost do everything the same.
The kids. On the weekends we play catch,
And the men come down and join us.
Then all of us go to the park and play some softball.
Every Saturday and Sunday is the same on that block.
Getting back to the old man,
I wish I could do something about that thing the cop
done, but
he wasn't the only one.
On 12th Street the same thing goes on with different
cops.
Everybody thinks
The cops stop stealing. How could they when they do it
themselves?
If you have money, every time you get busted, I bet
You could buy your way out of it.

Coco

*C*oco was fourteen and alcoholic. If he were turned loose with a dollar he would find someone to buy him a gallon of Bowery wine and he would get stoned. If someone gave him pills, he would take pills. If he could get grass, he would smoke. Anything, then, but dope. After all, he said, "I'm only fourteen."

He was wandering around the streets one night when I met him and took him home. No one was looking for him. His mother regularly locked him out of her apartment when she was entertaining or just felt like not being bothered and Coco often spent nights just wandering around the streets, sleeping, finally, in a boiler room, a hallway or with some compassionate stranger. Anyway, no one was looking for him tonight or any night.

He stayed for nearly a year, becoming part of our family, sharing with us his warmth and insights, and his problems.

He couldn't read. He couldn't tell time. He didn't know the alphabet. The only thing he knew for sure was his first and last name, and he couldn't spell them. And he had spent seven years of his life supporting the New York City public schools.

He couldn't see very well. The doctor we had examine him said that his was the first case of rickets he had ever seen. Coco's chest was concave. He never wanted to go to gym because he felt like a freak. But they made him go anyway and no one ever listened. He kept running away from school. No one knew why. His teacher told me he was a "nonintellectual" and seemed satisfied with that.

And he drank. Whenever he could he drank. Sometimes we managed to get him to go for as long as two weeks without being drunk, but then he'd see his mother in the street, she'd slip him a couple of words of discouragement and he'd be off and drinking. We tried not to get into the game, the alcoholic game that needs persecutors and good guys and guilt. We tried to make the rules clear and the rewards and punishments strong. And as long as he could put mama out of his head, he'd be okay.

But he was fourteen, and mama was still important, and we knew that we were just making the fuse a little longer, day by day a little longer, and we knew that that was all we could do.

A social worker from the welfare department came to call. It seemed that they were going to cut his mother's welfare because he wasn't living with her and she had told them to get him back with her so she could get her full allotment. Coco said no, he didn't want to go because she just drank up the money and he had no one to take care of him. The social worker suggested that he be put in a "protective environment" for his "own good." I asked her what she had in mind. And what she had in mind was the state mental hospital. In any case, she said, he couldn't go on with us. It was either back to his mama for the welfare money or into the state hospital. She left him with that decision.

Our fuse extending had come as far as it could. The bomb went off. Coco disappeared. We got a call the next night that he was drunk and in the street a few blocks away. I went to get him. When I came he was lying in the gutter. He was covered with dirt from his head to his feet. He was crying.

"I'm sorry Larry, I'm sorry," he kept saying and then pounded his fist or his head or his body into whatever he could for punctuation of his guilt and unhappiness.

"C'mon man, Coco," I said, "c'mon home."

He swung at me. He swung at me a lot, but somehow never hit me. We wrestled a lot, and I knew that was for hugging and being hugged and, occasionally, a test of strength. I always won. He was big and strong for his age, and sometime I think he let me win.

"C'mon Coco, c'mon Coco man, let's go home," I tried again.

"I ain't goin' to no fuckin' hospital," he cried.

"I know you ain't," I said, and took him home.

The city forgot about him for a while and we put Coco into a special reading school at NYU. He went every day and was starving to learn. He wasn't drinking. He slept with his books.

Two weeks later NYU dismissed him. It seems you

have to read at least third grade level to make it there. He was off the scale. So they kicked him out. We got him a tutor.

His tutor's name was Bob Bosworth and he was the best man in a one-to-one thing with a kid I have ever seen. He was gentle and he was solid. He taught Coco to read by walking with him and reading street signs. They stopped for coffee and the menu became reading text. They read the signs on the side of buses. Telephone booths. Movies, taxicabs, police phones, butcher shops, super markets, candy stores, liquor stores even. When Coco slept late, which wasn't often, Bob would go up to his room and wake him. Slowly, Coco got on the reading scale. He learned to write his name. He learned the alphabet. When we went out in the car he read every sign he could get. In the restaurants he would study the menu carefully.

"H-a-m and c-h-e-e-s-e—that's ham and cheese," he would say proudly and loudly. Very loudly.

And sometimes he would say ham and cheese when it read ham and swiss, but more often than not, he got it right on the nose. Other times he would test to make sure we were listening. Then when he saw we were, he would smile.

His drinking episodes were getting further and further apart.

By the time Coco was fifteen he was talking about going back into some kind of school. He was physically well, his feelings about himself had moved upward somewhat from zero, and he laughed a lot. Michelle had taken fifteen minutes a night for one week and taught him how to tell time and he wore a watch, offering the time to anyone he thought might be a little off schedule. I remember thinking that of all the changes he went through in the three years I had known him, the most important to him was that he could tell time.

His mother, in the meanwhile, had moved from place to place and for some time Coco couldn't find her. At one point he heard she went to Puerto Rico and that made him happy because there she would be with family. He talked about her more and more and the talk was warm and loving. He understood why she drank a lot and why it was hard for her to take care of him, he said, "It's hard to have kids by yourself."

When his mother returned to the scene, the social worker materialized with her.

"Coco will just have to go home," she said, "after all, she is his mother."

"Where has she been for the last year and a half?" I asked, not wanting to challenge her motherhood as much as her motives. "You know, no one's taken care of this kid since he was a baby?"

I heard both what I was saying and more. What had begun as a desperate move had become a tremendous investment. Coco had really become part of us and I was being bitchy about his mother. And resentful. I had done what all the books said not to do. I had gotten involved with a lost kid who needed some love.

But the fact of birth is incontestable. For whatever reasons she wanted him back with her, whatever her sins of neglect or indifference had been, she was Coco's mother. He knew it and we knew it.

So one day, just as he had come, Coco left without saying goodbye.

For a few months, as hard as we looked to spot him around the neighborhood we couldn't find him. His mother lived nearby and no one was ever home. Coco just disappeared.

More than a year went by. I heard that Coco was back on the bottle, but I never saw him. Kids said he was in pretty bad shape but that he wasn't around much. He was spending a lot of time in Brooklyn. Some thought he might have put himself in the hospital. We couldn't find out.

One night nearly three years after the social worker sent Coco home the buzzer buzzed and I went to the window to see who it was. It was Coco and he was drunk. He was banging on the front door of our building and our landlady was screaming at him to stop or she would call the police. Infuriated, he was trying to break down the door as I came down.

I opened the door and went out to him. He was really torn up. He was much bigger than the last time I had seen him. He was already eighteen. His eyes were glassy as if he had taken a lot of pills with his wine.

"Larry, man . . ." he said, barely able to stand on his own.

"Larry man, I'm a junkie. A goddam junkie. Look at me man. I'm all fucked up."

I sat down on the stoop with him and put my arm around him. We cried a little, but he was too stoned to talk to. He just wanted to talk and he came to do that.

"Remember Bob Bosworth?" he asked, reeling and not waiting for an answer.

"He really gave a shit about me."

"Yeah. He did," I said.

"Y'know, I wish I could go back and do that again. That was the bestest time in my life. That Bosworth, man, he sure could teach."

The message was delivered. Coco got up and smiled and walked away. I watched him stumble down the street and around the corner.

Schools

Kids feel that they are a captive in someone else's game. And captive they are. Compulsory education has become the legal tool by which children are forced into The System. Although every major million-dollar study has confirmed what a simple (free) conversation with a kid could have provided, that poor kids' schools do active damage to active minds, children are still forced by law and order to attend under penalty of jail.

Under the cover of "Doing What's Best For Our Children" the public education system has been allowed to degenerate to something akin to a part-time prison camp while the legal pressure for kids to stay increases.

A child from the age of seven can be locked in jail in New York City for rejecting the destruction he faces daily in school. He can be put into the cruelest of jails without even the guarantees of that Constitution he may have heard about because he was self-protective enough to want to leave a place that kills his mind and confines his body. Cruel and unusual punishment. But could you ever dream of a principal being put in jail because that same kid never learned to read? Or never learned the alphabet past the letter F? Or never learned to tell time? No one can believe that. But a child is jailed for failure to tolerate his captors and it isn't seen as absurd. Even though in wartime a soldier is bound by duty to escape from his enemies if he can and in the poor kids' schools it is always wartime.

Power wins wars and children are held punishable for the failure of the schools because children are powerless. And it is this powerlessness of children, poor children and their families, that for the most part explains the failure of the schools.

No one does anything, according to the bureaucratic ethic, that he doesn't have to do. And the schools have not had to teach children. The children have had to be present and teachers have had to be paid. But the schools have not had to teach.

Captive means being trapped against your will in a place that is not where your instincts tell you to be with people who care nothing for you but have a vested interest in your captivity. That is what public education for street kids has become. And as long as teachers' unions and Boards of Education are allowed to work in collusion lining their pockets and enhancing their position with the spoils of this war against the children, then the children will continue to die. Some while attempting to escape.

Leo

How dead is a man's soul
When he lives a life of toys
How dead is a man's soul
When he lives the life of a decoy
How dead is all these joys
When a man is a boy

Leo wrote that when he was sixteen. If you knew Leo, you would have to say that it would be a fitting epitaph. But he's not dead yet.

Death crept up on Leo early. His father abandoned the family when Leo was twelve. When he was thirteen he was taking care of his five brothers and sisters while his mother was away, so Leo never had much time to hang out with the guys. He lost himself in books and in junior high school played in all the plays. He knew Shakespeare's tragedies but ignored modern literature and he knew of far-off exotic places while ignoring more local geography. But no one put it together that

Leo longed to be born in another time or in another place. No one knew how badly he wanted out of his life. He was a Puerto Rican Prince Hamlet.

At sixteen he busted out. After nearly four years of confinement as the substitute parent of his little brothers and sisters, Leo came home to his apartment and found his mother had given his dog away to the pound to be killed.

"We just can't afford it anymore," his mother said, "and besides, it was getting in the way." His mother had married a man who Leo knew was a junkie and Leo blamed the fact that there wasn't enough in the house to eat on the fact that his new stepfather wasn't working and was taking all the money around to buy dope. But Leo didn't squeal on his new stepfather. It was against his ethics.

"And another thing," his mother added, "what the hell are you doing taking dope? I found this in the bathroom!" She handed him an empty glassine envelope, the kind that heroin comes packaged in.

"I'm not takin' no dope," Leo said sullenly, knowing who had left the envelope behind.

His mother slapped his face. It was the slap that meant both his freedom and his doom.

He ran out the door and down the stairs of the tenement building. When he came to the front door he ran through the glass panel cutting his arm badly. He was bleeding and screaming and crying and running when a cop spotted him and called an ambulance. While they were bandaging his deeply cut arm, they began asking him questions and Leo ran out of the emergency room with the cops in full pursuit. Maybe, they figured, this kid was involved in some kind of crime. Maybe he was high on something. Maybe he was just a nut. So when he ran, they ran after him.

Still bleeding and stopping somewhere on the way for a handful of pills and a bottle, Leo made it all the way from Brooklyn to Harlem where his father lived. He found his father's building and ran inside and pounded on the door. His father's new woman opened the door and saw Leo, the condition he was in, and called Leo's father. He came to the door and without commenting on Leo's injury or his agitation said simply, "What are you doing here?"

"You gotta help me," Leo cried. "We don't have any food at home and the guy momma's with takes dope around the kids and they got rid of my dog an . . ."

His father shrugged and closed the door leaving Leo in the middle of his plea.

Now, miles out of his own territory, his head spinning from loss of blood, speed, Four Roses, terror, rage, and rejection, Leo called for help.

He had given a stranger a dime and my number and asked the stranger to call me and in this most cynical, unfriendly, and uncaring city, the stranger did just that.

"You Larry Cole?" the voice on the phone asked.

It was 3:00 A.M. and about all I knew for sure was that I was Larry Cole.

"Unghuh."

"There's this guy on 127th and Broadway who's tore up pretty bad. He's raising all kinds of hell and he's got a knife. You better hurry and get him before someone else does."

"Thanks a lot," I told the samaritan, interpreting that the "someone else" meant the police.

Less than twenty minutes later I was in Harlem at 127th and Broadway and Leo was in the middle of a small circle of onlookers, menacing them with a knife, not seeing anyone or anything he knew and looking like a cornered lion. "Leo the lion," I thought, but it wasn't funny. His face was twisted, his bloody bandage dangled grotesquely from his arm, his eyes were frantic. The people in the circle stayed their distance and warned me, when they saw me coming close, to stay away.

"Stay away, man, this guy's spaced out."

I made sure Leo recognized me before I went through the imaginary wall of the circle. I asked him for the knife, he gave it to me, I asked him to get into the car, he did, and we drove downtown. Home.

We gave Leo some hot soup and put him to bed on the sofa.

The next morning we talked about the night before. Leo filled me in on all the details, no food or milk for his brothers and sisters, the destruction of his dog, the false accusation, the slashing of his arm, escaping from the police, the cold rejection by his father. He had lived a lifetime of psychological disaster in only a few short hours.

His mother called the next day and wanted to know where Leo was.

"I don't know what's the matter with him," she told me, "he ran out of here like a crazy man. My husband and I, we're just gonna have him locked up or something."

The more she talked the more I understood Leo's dilemma. Forced to live in a building the landlord had abandoned, without heat, hot water, or services because she couldn't find another apartment that would fit into her welfare requisites, she tried to make a little on the side working in a beauty shop. She couldn't tell the welfare department because then they would take what she made out of her already impossible budget. That was welfare department policy. No one busts out.

Left without a husband for years and still a young woman herself she was trapped with all those kids in that apartment and, yes, she said, she did put a lot of that burden on Leo, she did go out and have some fun.

"But he is the oldest," she said, "and it is his responsibility."

Her message for me to deliver to Leo was this: He either comes home and acts nice and gets back in the bridle or she would have the cops looking for him. He was, she said, a wayward minor.

But our wayward minor had other ideas.

Leo the romantic saw himself rushing off to the Yukon to make his fortune, sailing off on a merchant ship, high-balling it on a cross-country freight. Leo the realist went down to enlist in the Marines.

He lied about his age and they turned him down anyway, he had an old bone deformity from a never set broken arm a few years before. He was depressed as hell. He couldn't even give his life away.

So he got his own apartment. He worked part time and went to school part time determined to finish school and become independent. His mother never called after that first day and Leo figured that since she was convinced he wasn't going to be her full-time babysitter anymore she wouldn't be any more trouble. He was right. What he didn't figure was that the freedom he now thought he had, the straight line to the promised land that he thought he was now following, carried a lot of ghosts. It was no time at all before these ghosts were eating him alive, pushing him, pulling him, tearing him up inside.

However he felt about his mother and her threats, however he felt about his father abandoning him, there was still the fact of his brothers and sisters, hungry and cold at home. It offered no consolation that he was getting himself into a position where he could really help them. They were now, their suffering now, and all the rationalizations in the world couldn't change that.

So as often as he could, when he was sure his mother wasn't around, he went home to see the kids, bringing them something and feeding his guilt each time he left, since whatever he was ever to bring them could never be enough.

The Yukon and Dangerous Dan McGrew, standing at the helm of a merchant ship sailing into South Sea waters, living the life of Dylan's songs, hitching freights, shipping out to fight America's enemies, making his fortune, and coming back to a land where mothers can love and care for their young, and fathers never run away, and little brothers and sisters never have to cry for milk or from cold or loneliness. Those were Leo's nighttime dreams and daytime fantasies.

But underneath the adolescent dreams of freedom and heroics, behind the wishes to live, be strong and miraculous, a Hamlet bubbled and churned inside of Leo, questioning and challenging his existence.

Whether to be or not became Leo's riddle and he solved it in his own way.

He took his trip to another place, he sailed off on that merchant ship and found the land of painless

oblivion not with a quickness of his Hamlet's dagger, but in keeping with his real time and his real place, he found a slower death in drugs.

Leo is still alive, paying his way on drugs as a police informant on other kids with other mothers and vaguely remembered fathers—as ". . . he lives the life of a decoy . . . when a man is a boy."

School on the Lower East, when I was 11 or 12

First of all the schools in New York are fucked up. I remember when I went to public school. You had to wear a tie every day to school. I didn't know what learning had to do with the way you dress. When I would go to classes they would put me in the back of the room and I would feel like nothing. I had a lot of ideas to throw out, but (she) the teacher, made believe that I wasn't even in the class. So I got mad and I started to playing around in class, then the teacher gets up tight, and says, "You! In the back." "Who me?" "Yes, you, Mr. Burgos. You are always making noise, and I am tired of talking to you about making noise." I answered, "I am always put in the back of the fucking room."

Teacher: You did and said something that I didn't like.

Eddie: Fuck you! You been putting me in the back for three fuckin' months with a paper tie on me making me look like a fool. How would you like me to put you in the back and I would be the teacher?

Teacher: I wouldn't be there in the first place.

Eddie: Why, because you think you're better than me? You fuckin'—

Teacher: All right you are going to the dean.

As I walk out I say "Thanks a lot you cop." Now I am in the dean's office. He said, "Alright Eddie you've been here before for the same thing in class and I'm tired of seeing your face in this room."

Eddie: You think I don't get tired of seeing your face?

Dean: Nice going, what you said.

Eddie: I know it's nice what I said.

WHAP—right across my face. I turn and look at him and say, "Don't worry I'll pay you back." Whap! Again he hit me in my face. This time I couldn't turn around and look at him, I just took my hand out of my pocket and punched him across his face. Then we started to fight in the room. He banged my head on the wall then I fell down on the floor, then he picked me up and said, "I'm sorry about what happened." I said to myself 'He is trying to sweet charm me,' then I said in a loud voice, "Fuck you!," and ran out.

And I didn't go back to school for a long time. Besides, I didn't go back because I wasn't learning anything in school, and besides, they don't teach you what you want to learn, They teach you what They want you to learn.

The cop and I

One day on a Friday I didn't go to school. I was with 3 of my boys. We all got together and we left to the park. We played basketball for a while, then we all put in money to buy a bottle of wine and some smoke. Fred said to me, "Eddie, let's get some girls and bring them up to my house."

Eddie: That's cool, let's do that.

Fred: Alright, you look for some, and I'll look at the other side of the park and we'll meet here at 11:30 A.M.

O.K. now one hour had passed. Now it's 11:30 A.M.

I come first to the park, without any girls, I say to myself, "God damn. I couldn't find any girls to have fun with, but that's alright I know Freddie will bring some girls." Now I see Freddie across from the park.

Eddie: Hey Freddie, you found some girls?

Fred: Yeah, I found some girls.

Eddie: But where are they?

Fred: I said I found them, but I didn't bring any with me.

Eddie: But why not?

Fred: Cause they said they wouldn't come because their mother said not to stick around with bad guys.

Eddie: How in the fuck would their mother see them with us?

Fred: You know they got some big mouths around here.

Eddie: Fuck the big mouths around here, and besides, today is my birthday and I want a girl to warm me up.

Fuck all this talk, I'm going into the school to get me one. Are you coming with me?

Fred: Yeah, I'll go with you.

As I walk up to the stairs of the school this big ass cop comes up.

Cop: Hey you, where the hell you think you're going.

Eddie: I'm going into the school.

Cop: You can't go into the school.

Fred: Why not?

Cop: Cause you are too late.

Eddie: So I'll get a late pass.

Cop: You heard what I said.

Eddie: You cops are all alike.

Cop: Come over here.

He took me by my neck, squeezing me real tight.

Fred: Let go of him, you're hurting him.

He threw me down the stairs.

Eddie: You big ass fucking cop.

He ran after me and Fred. We started to run to the park. I slipped and he came right behind me and caught me, but Freddie got away. He was slapping me all over the place. He kicked me up my ass and pulled my hair.

Cop: Listen you little punk, if you ever call me any names again I'll see that you get put away.

I started to cry.

Eddie: I'll bet you wouldn't hit my father like that, because you know he would kick your fuckin' ass.

Cop: What did you say?

Eddie: I said I bet you my father would kick me up my ass if he caught me doing what I was doing, that's what I said.

Cop: O.K. I'll let you go this time, but next time you know what will happen to you.

Eddie: I know what would happen to me next time, I would get my ass kicked again. (I said that in a low voice.)

Cop: What did you say?

Eddie: "I said, I'll go to school again." I was afraid to say it again because he would smack me across my head.

Cop: O.K. go home you little punk.

As he let my hand go I started to run, and said, "You," but as I turned my head, in front of me I saw two cops, and I said, "Thank you for letting me go," but as I was going home I was sounding the fuck out of him.

Next day comes, I meet Freddie in the park.

Fred: What happened to you?

Eddie: Nothing.

Fred: What you mean nothing.

Eddie: Just what I said, nothing. I fucked him up.

Fred: Oh yeah! Boy Eddie, you got a lot of nerve.

Eddie: I know I did, that's why I got bumps in my head. Anyway, let's forget about this, let's go to the park and have some fun.

Hitching the bus to the Village

One Monday morning me and my boys got together with our bikes and tipped to The Village. We would hold on to the bus, on the side, to ride faster. We would get off our bikes and go into the stores to cop something. While I'm talking to the clerk and keeping him busy, my friend Jose would be putting things in his pocket.

Jose: Let's tip Eddie.

Eddie: I'll be right up, Jose.

So now we meet outside of the store.

Eddie: What did you take?

Jose: Only some combs and some pens and some other bullshit.

Jimmy: That's all you took?

Eddie: You fuckin' liar, you have some more things on you.

Jose: But I don't have anything else.

Jimmy: Let's search him.

Jose: I have some boys, you guys can't even trust me.

Eddie: We don't want you to take that change.

We looked into his pocket and we found 5 tubes of glue.

Jimmy: Didn't you say you didn't have anything else?

Jose: Yeah, I forgot to tell you I had 5 tubes on me, which I took from the store.

Eddie: Now you tell me, after all this time.

We got on our bikes and we tipped. As we would ride next to ladies in the street, for each one we saw, we would grab their ass, ladies would jump up "sky high" and start yelling. We could hear the ladies from blocks away. The cop ran after us, he caught me. He took me to a lady to see if I was the one who did it. The lady said, "Yeah, that's the one who did it, that nasty little boy."

Eddie: That means you won't let little boys grab it, but you will let men grab it.

Cop: Stop getting smart.

Eddie: Oh, you just want some off her.

Cop: One more smart remark out of you and I'm taking you to the station.

Eddie: Alright, I won't get smart again.

Cop: Why do you do those things to the ladies, answer that.

Eddie: Alright, I'm going to answer, but believe me I'm not trying to get smart with what I'm going to say.

Cop: Would you get to the point and say why you did it.

Eddie: Well I did it because she was walking down

the sidewalk shaking her ass left and right, I just wanted to feel it.

Lady: I can't listen to this anymore, he's crazy.

Eddie: Miss, believe me, I am not crazy. If I was, you'd be crazy after I finished with you.

Cop: Let's go, I'm taking you to your parents.

Eddie: Wait! Can I ask you a question before you take me home?

Cop: Yeah?

Eddie: If you saw something like that shaking right in front of your eyes, what would you do?

The cop mumbled a few words.

Cop: I wouldn't do anything.

Eddie: I wonder who your wife is, she must have problems with you, you faggot.

He had me by the hand, I swung my hand and he turned me loose, and I ran to my bike and cut out.

As I was riding my bike away, real fast, I turned to see the two fools (the cop and the lady) at the corner debating their heads off. My friends were waiting for me in the park.

Jose: I thought you'd never come.

Jimmy: I knew he was coming. For a tube of glue he'd do anything.

Squealing: in the crowd

When me and my boys pull something, there always was one out of the crowd to squeal to the cops, but we never could find out who it was. One day we robbed a candy store, but the guy who always squeals, he was in it too. After we did that, we found out who it was, so me and my friend, Sam, we took him to the yard. Smack. He started to cry, "I didn't say anything to the man in the candy store."

Eddie: You are lying to us.

Jimmy: You already hit me enough, why don't you leave me alone and let me go.

Sam: Eddie, let's let him go.

Eddie: But why?

Sam: No reason, just let him go.

Eddie: Alright, he's a punk anyway, we don't need him.

Jimmy ran home crying. Me and my friend Sam went home.

The next day comes.

I came downstairs around 2:30 P.M. I saw all my friends, and we had a game of stick ball. After a while the people and the cops chased us out of the block.

Cops: Go to the park, there's lots of room.

Eddie: We're too tired to walk down there.

Sam: Forget about them, let's go some place else, and do something where nobody can stop us.

So we went to the park. We played basketball for a while, then we saw these white boys. They gave us bad looks and we didn't dig that. One of the white boys called out, "Hey you hicks."

We turned our heads and we all walked over there. We grabbed one by the shirt and all of them jumped in the fight, so we jumped in too. My friend Sam picked up a baseball bat and hit one of them in his back with it. They got up and started to run. We ran after them but we couldn't find them, so we all went home.

The next day came.

I saw this girl taking a leak. I ran downstairs to the yard.

Eddie: What are you doing there?

She jumped up and said, "Nothing, I'm just throwing some junk out."

Eddie: Oh yeah, sure didn't seem that way.

I walked next to her.

Eddie: You sure look pretty.

I put my hands around her and I held her tight. I kissed her. She kissed me back. I was a little bit shakey and nervous. I slid my hand down her back slowly. I pulled down her zipper and started to feel her you know what. She took my hand and pulled it up.

Eddie: Come on, let me do it just a little bit.

Girl: No, because somebody might come in.

I was getting mad.

Eddie: Motherfucker! I want some of that.

Girl: Some of what?

Eddie: Motherfucker, between your legs, before I tell everybody who you did it with.

Girl: O.K., I'll let you do it, if you don't tell nobody.

Eddie: Don't worry, I won't tell nobody.

I pulled down her dress. All of a sudden my friend runs in the yard.

Sam: Eddie, there's a cop behind me.

Eddie: That's a fine time for that! You blew everything just when I was getting to business. She just ran up the stairs.

Sam: I was just playing around, no cop was coming behind me.

Eddie: So why did you say the cop was coming?

Sam: Because I wanted a piece of pussy too.

Eddie: But couldn't you fucking wait till I finished.

Sam: No.

Eddie: What you mean, no.

Sam: Cause I didn't want to go last.

Eddie: I had her first.

Sam: So what does that mean? You have to go first because you seen her first.

Eddie: You got some fucking nerve.

Sam: I know I have some nerve, that's why I did it.

Eddie: Now we both don't have her.

Sam: You think I don't know that.

Eddie: I'm glad you know that, you creep.

Sam: Who the fuck are you calling a creep.

Eddie: You! Who else?

Sam: Oh yeah!

Sam: If you think I'm a creep, do something about it.

Eddie: I will.

We started to fight. We threw each other around. The same girl comes down to the yard.

Girl: Stop fighting!

We stopped fighting for a while. We both looked at each other and we grabbed her. We fucked around with her. We grabbed her pussy, her ass and had a beautiful time, then she cut out to her house. We both put our hands around each other and walked out of the yard, nice and cool.

Eddie: Tomorrow, Sam.

Sam: Yeah, O.K., in the morning.

Loretta

Loretta walked into LEAP without her usual pasted-on smile. For her, its absence was more of a signal of emergency and of pain than most other people's hysteria. Her expression was that of badly hidden terror, the kind that movie heroines showed just after the Gestapo had torn their finger nails out in those unsuccessful attempts to get them to talk. Casually, almost smilingly, she told Michelle, "I just ran away from home."

"Why?"

"My father came in and he called he a hoor. So I said, 'how come you call me that?' And he hit me over the head with a coke bottle."

Michelle looked at her head and there was a deep cut hidden in her long black hair. As Loretta spoke, she began to shake. A trickle of blood was dripping onto her skirt (four sizes too big), and onto the floor. Michelle washed the cut and made a quick compress.

"What happened baby?" Michelle asked. She hugged Loretta.

"What happened?"

As Loretta began to answer, I thought of what I already knew of her family. Her father and two of her three brothers were junkies. Her mother did anything to keep the old man from killing the kids, while at the same time fighting to keep an image of respectability in the neighborhood. It was the image of respectability that kept her periodically strong and sane enough to protect the lives of her daughters.

Loretta also had three sisters: the oldest, away from home when she was sixteen after being sexually attacked by her father, was now married and living in Brooklyn. I met her once and she told me that the old man had raped, or tried to, each of the other girls, and that the girls were always running to her.

"I don't know what I can do," she said to me then. "I got no room and my husband don't wanna get into a whole thing. Besides, when my mother finds out where they are, she sends the police for them and we don't wanna get into a lotta trouble."

I tuned back into the now. To Loretta. Shaking more, sobbing, telling Michelle what happened.

"After he hit me with the bottle, I fell on the kitchen floor and Pat (her youngest sister) cried for him to stop. He picked up a wire hanger and pulled my blouse off and started to beat me with it."

She showed swollen raw welts on her back. Later she showed Michelle welts and bruises over her entire body.

"I screamed and Pat ran to get my mother. Then he

ran and got the broom and started pushing the broom handle into me . . . into my . . . you know. . . ."

Loretta stopped. The crying stopped. She just began to shake, and Michelle pulled her close.

"Go ahead and cry baby," Michelle coaxed. But Loretta chose to take it all inside and her sobs were seen as random constrictions of her body as she lay in Michelle's arms.

Michelle looked up at me standing helplessly by.

"We've got to do something," she said for lack of something to say.

"I know," I answered, for the same reason.

It was 1963 and all I knew about the world of protective institutions I read in books or saw in the movies. LEAP hadn't yet developed its own network of helpers and I was on my own to find out which, if any, public body could be called now to save Loretta from what was obviously a clear and present danger to her life.

I called the SPCC. The Society for the Prevention of Cruelty to Children, an old-line social service agency whose lines to the police and the courts, I had been told, were strong. Very strong. So I called the SPCC.

After an unusual amount of buck passing and shunting around they rang one of the caseworkers. I told her about Loretta, the history of the family, and even how the old man was wanted by Ohio authorities for running out on a rape charge. She listened. I told her about the beatings, about the coke bottle and the split head, how the neighbors witnessed the periodic attacks, about the junkie thing and she listened. But when I told her about the broomstick episode she stopped listening. I actually *heard* her stop listening. It was like a click of silence and from her next comment I knew she had, all at once, turned off, rewound, and erased.

"You should have let the parents know where she is. They are the parents you know."

"Look. What about the girl," I said. "We've got to do something to protect her. I don't give a damn about what I should have done."

"Okay Mr. Cole. Why don't you send the girl in. We'll talk to her and make some kind of determination."

"I'll bring her in myself."

"Well, okay. Now what did you say her name was? Her address? Her father's name. . . ."

"Hey. Wait," I said. "You're not going to turn her over to *them* are you?"

"No. You needn't worry about that. We just have to have as much information as possible before she comes in just in case she's too shy or scared to give us the information for our records."

When we arrived at the SPCC, that official agency with those direct connections to the Family Court, we waited on the usual wooden benches for an hour until a woman came out and asked Loretta to come with her. I got up to come in and was told I would have to wait outside. Loretta panicked and wanted to leave.

So did I.

They finally agreed that I could join her for the interview.

"We only want what's best for the girl," the usher lady oozed.

It was then that I knew I made the wrong choice. It

was like when somebody says, "Trust me. Just trust me." You can be sure that you're being had.

Without so much as a smile or the faintest glimmer of warmth, what came next, billed as "An Interview," was what I was to find only a typical example of guilt and pain infliction under the cloak of official inquest.

"Well why did your father call you that?" (a hoor) the social worker challenged.

"Cause I got home after 3. I got home at 3:30 and I was with a boy," Loretta swallowed her answer.

"Well he is your father and you are only thirteen. Do you think you should be going with boys?"

"Look lady," I said, "she didn't say anything about *going with* boys. She said she was with a boy. And that's not the issue anyway. Do you see this cut? Do you see these welts? Why are you putting her through this kind of questioning?"

"Now, that's exactly why we didn't want you in here," Miss Socialworker clucked. "If you keep this up. . . ."

She was interrupted by a knock on the door. Another lady out of the same mold, angry face and tight body, came in and motioned our investigator to come outside.

The door opened and they beckoned for Loretta. And as it opened all the way we could see into the next office.

There, seated stiffly next to the desk were Loretta's parents.

Twenty minutes later, after everyone but me telling Loretta what a terrible thing she had done, embarrassing her parents like this, her sacrificing, hard-working, well-intentioned parents, Loretta was sent home in her father's custody.

It was little comfort to know that she managed to separate me from the conspiracy.

"They are your parents," our social worker repeated as Loretta was led out held firmly by the elbow, "and you should try to make them happy."

Police, courts, and corruption

Street kids don't share the outsider's blind belief in the existence of justice. One reason is that they are educated by what they see, not what they are told, and what they see is that justice in America carries a price tag. And unlike other shabby merchandise brought into their streets for one last try at sale before it hits the garbage dump, whatever frayed and torn justice that may be for sale to the poor is not similarly discounted.

According to David Burnham, a *New York Times* reporter who has been close to the study of police corruption both at the *Times* and with the President's Crime Commission, "the ten thousand or so small Puerto Rican grocery stores scattered around N.Y. City pay an estimated 6 million dollars a year in payoffs to the police in order to stay open on Sunday." That means that each of these small "mom and pop" operations pay an average of six hundred dollars each year for the privilege of making a living, mostly due to the exist-

ence of a Sunday "blue law" or closing law that nearly
everyone in the city has been against for the past half
century. It might be asked to whose interest it is to keep
this law on the books.

In one precinct in Spanish Harlem, Burnham estimated that twenty million dollars was spent in illegal
gambling each year, "a good part of which," he says,
"goes to the police." And not very many people are interested in keeping gambling illegal and in the hands of
the syndicate either. Except for whoever is keeping it
that way.

The biggest joke to street kids is when government
officials make statements about cleaning up on dope
traffic or corruption. There are really only two groups
of people who benefit financially from the illegality of
drugs: the big-time importer and distributor, and officials who are supposed to stop import and distribution.
The pusher on the street usually makes enough for his
own habit, to support himself. And if anyone has to be
sacrificed to the periodic "crackdowns" it's going to be
him. But the big-time guys and the cops have a mar-
riage made in heaven.

Storekeepers, bookies, numbers runners, drug ped-
dlers, prostitutes, landlords, building superintendents,
and others easily intimidated by a policeman's strict
adherence to the laws and regulations of the city, pay.
And pay. And pay. It has gone on for so long and become such a natural part of the routine of the police
department, that there are often not even minimal
efforts made to keep it hidden. Members of the President's Crime Commission, identified as such and traveling with city policemen, found that nearly one-third of
the officers observed in the normal course of their duty

committed either felony or misdemeanor offenses or openly admitted to doing so.

Kids whose lives are spent on the street, whose threat to the security of the police is certainly less than that of a presidential representative, see even more, as you might expect. And anyone who tells street kids about the honesty or virtue of The Law, is telling them more about his own ignorance than anything else. Teachers, social workers, and other outsiders are in the forefront of the kids' daily confrontation with absurdity: people telling them not to believe their own eyes.

Without police corruption, it would be almost impossible for the present conditions of drug abuse to exist. Big-time importers and distributors would be in prison and the billions of dollars a year in blood money they are taking in lives and property and wasted potential could be used to renew the cities. It has been estimated that it costs society $100,000 per year for each junkie. This for what he has to steal to keep up his habit, what it costs in police man-hours, court costs, jail and prison costs, as well as the destruction of property and neighborhoods where drugs are rampant and the loss of each drug addict's participation in the nation's work force.

In New York City alone there are over 100,000 junkies. Ten billion dollars a year lost in New York City alone.

It is no coincidence that the interest in controlling drug abuse mushroomed when the drugs started to reach the children of the suburbs, the children of the believers. The lives of street kids have been sacrificed to the dollar sign for over a decade without so much as a whimper from outsiders. Now that the infection is spreading out of control, the affluent are being educated, slowly, about the reasons, the diseases of corruption and malfeasance. Maybe in a few years they'll hear the message of their children. Too late.

Certainly the alienation of the young is a root cause of addiction. But isn't it just possible that the very corruption that allows them to buy their drugs is, at the same time, at the root of their alienation? Would kids, either on the street or on the college campus, have so much to escape from if the institutions around them were not so blatantly corrupt? And their parents so deaf, dumb, and blind?

For street kids, corruption is expected. Anyone who comes in contact with them who claims not to be corrupt is suspect. A fool even. Kind of like the way most of Middle America would look at a guy who didn't cheat "just a little bit" on his income tax or who didn't offer the traffic cop ten bucks in order to save a fine of fifty. Street kids don't understand the concept of honest cops because they haven't known one.

Each week a police car pulls up in front of a particular building; a building that everyone knows houses the local bookie. And each week one cop goes in while his partner waits in the car. And each week the cop comes out with a brown paper bag. And each week kids watch until finally they don't even see it anymore. It just becomes part of the background.

The kids see my initial reaction to what is going on before my own eyes. The eyes of a once-believer.

"I don't believe it," I say as I watch a cop come out of a Puerto Rican market on Avenue C, counting his money. "I just don't believe he could take a payoff in broad daylight."

"What do you think then," one kid says, "you think he's counting his change?"

Everyone laughs.

I watch one day as a car, a flashy Cadillac with easily identifiable upstate plates, pulls up to the corner of Avenue C and 4th Street and drops a large package to a man waiting on the corner. Just like the kids told me, this is the corner where "drops" are made. The corner where the area peddler gets his merchandise from the wholesaler. Right out in the open.

I watch as the man everyone told me is the neighborhood distributor to about fifty or so pushers takes the package and goes into the luncheonette. I watch all of this in broad daylight and all taking place no more than twenty feet from two uniformed policemen.

This was in 1964 and although I had spent some months with kids on the street, I was still a believer down deep. I still believed in the rotten apple theory of corruption. You know the gambit. "There's a few bad apples in any large organization but that doesn't mean the whole barrel is rotten." The liberal catechism. Institutions are never rotten. Only a few individuals. Belief in that catechism gives them hope. Periodically they purge some poor corrupt slob and his blood satisfies them. Sometimes I think the organization keeps a few dummies just for such living sacrifice. They know that they can keep people happy by, from time to time, throwing the reformers a few bodies. Better that than for anyone to take the responsibility (or the risk) of attempting to clean up the whole schmeer.

And so, being of sound mind and body, and a public-spirited citizen, and not knowing that those two states have become contradictory, outraged at the thought of kids believing that *all* cops were on the take, and more outraged to think they may be right—in all this confusion I decided to test my faith. I went to see the captain of the precinct.

Now, I wasn't very street wise, but I also wasn't an out and out dummy. So when I went to the captain with my little bit of info on the car and the drop spot, complete with license numbers and badge numbers and descriptions, I carefully instructed him not to connect my name in any way with the information. He went through all the dramatics of the television police stories. He would keep my name in the strictest confidence.

"Thanks for bringing this matter to my attention," said the Captain. "You can count on me to keep you out of it."

I didn't have to count long. For two months after my attempt at anonymous heroics, I got threatening phone calls at home.

"Y' tink yer funny, big mout, goin to the cops wit yer lies. Y' tryin to get people in trouble? Y'll get yerself in trouble. That's who." Bad imitations of movie hood talk.

"Read tomorrow morning's paper. There's a story in it about some guy who was a rat and got killed."

And so it went on.

Until I got the point. There was only one person beside me who knew that I spoke to the Captain about the narcotics drop. That was the Captain. So I never talked to him about anything anymore. And by that single decision I stopped being a believer.

I found out later from a friend who is a cop that a "nut" or payoff envelope of $2000 per month per man, in the middle echelons of the police, is pretty standard. Not bad for just looking the other way. I let my imagination tell me how much they might make for actually *doing* something. And I began to understand how this all affects the kids on the street who watch cops and justice being bought and sold.

I'm sitting over a drink with a lawyer friend who's telling me about a case he's in. His client is a young homosexual whose sex life and habits have been active enough for him to be "known" to the local police. He has had a standing "agreement" with them for some time and hasn't been hassled.

Then one night, cops come busting into his house and arrest him. They charge him with running an immoral house or something. He calls my friend from the precinct and asks him to come down and defend him. "I don't know what the hell this is all about," the arrested man cries indignantly to his lawyer, "I've been blowing everyone in the place who wanted me. We had an agreement."

What bothered me most about the story was that the arrested young man thought more of the betrayal than of his ongoing persecution; the price he had to pay to live his life. The kids would say he did what he had to do to live. Some dues.

So when kids on the street told me that they went to a transvestite party to get some free smoke and saw some local cops there joining in the transvestivities, and they told me that as casually as you might mention part of the guest list of any party, I wasn't shocked or surprised.

"What do you think they do with the pot they grab from us?" one kid challenges. "Flush it down the toilet?"

The kids slapped five and laughed.

I couldn't resist. "You mean they don't flush it down the toilet?"

It's a strange truth that even though kids know that cops are on the make and on the take, that they go where the money is and that most of them don't Give-A-Damn about the neighborhood except what they can shake out of it, many still respect the police as men, because, after all, they share very much the same values. Make it where you can, however you can, whenever you can, but make it. Cops respect the kids in a funny way too, because they know the kids are smart, street smart, like they were when they were kids and like they are now as grown-up men in blue.

When it comes to war, of course, the cops in the long run win. They have the artillery, the equipment, The Law behind them. But in their day-to-day confrontations in the street, behind the mutual racial epithets and the surface hatred, there is a strange kind of empathy. Kind of like a mutual understanding that all of them come from the same stew, that they are all products of the same ethic, that they are all victims of a higher corruption. Only outsiders see cops and street kids as natural enemies. The fact is that they are enemies. Circumstances make that so. But there is nothing natural about it.

Cops and kids are caught up in the racial struggle just like the rest of the country. They clash more often, so it is easy to point to when you need fuel to prove that the fires of race hate are burning fiercely. But while there are some "racist" cops and while there are some kids who really do hate anything white, the majority of street kids would probably get along well with the majority of cops if both of them weren't being so actively pitted against each other by the people who gain from such diversionary maneuvers.

Cops are taught to hate the kids and to think and refer to them as "animals" by people who need a scared and edgy police department as well as people who need to justify their own failures. Their education is like the education of teachers. What they learn formally turns out to mean nothing. When they really begin to learn is when for the first time an old-time teacher pushes up next to them in the lunch room and says:

"I saw you with your animals today. Gave you a hard time, eh? Well, you'll learn. They act like animals, you treat them like animals. You gotta learn to use your hands. You gotta learn, you're not in a school. You're in a zoo."

And just like with that teacher, who either accepts the zoo concept or gets the hell out, the young cop learns the language of fear from his elders who have a like need to destroy the idealism of the young and eager for fear of having their own guilt and incompetence exposed.

The kids learn race hate too. And they learn to hate cops. A lot of what they learn is firsthand and real. Most cops treat street kids like street litter. But a lot of their response to cops is similar to their response to white storekeepers. They are white and they are on their street, and there is enough exploitation by them to release the hatred and frustration caused by the oppression of whites *who they don't see,* people who they can never get back at. And cops get the brunt of this.

Cops are on their way up the class ladder. Most

have ditched the lower class or the lower middle class and have the hang-ups associated with such a scramble. White cops, like a lot of their black and brown counterparts, find it hard to look back at where they came from. Most of them aren't working as cops because they get some kind of delight out of cracking young black or Spanish heads. They are working for a house in the suburbs, a new Detroit car, and a pension. The chaos caused by the political system, the social conditions that have created hungry, angry, sick, exploited, and uneducated kids, unemployed and "unemployable," is just a fact to complicate their new-found entrance to the middle class—the world of installment affluence. Poverty, for the majority of cops, is not something they came out of with any understanding. It is something they have passed through, and something that *now* threatens their life and their security.

So the cops and the kids walk through the streets as enemies. But they are both players in someone else's game.

It's always funny to me to sit in court and see kids talking to their arresting officer like they were brothers. Sometimes they go outside in the hall and I listen to them.

"Why you hangin' around with the bums?" the cop would say, "they get you into trouble and where the hell are they? Some friends. You're a good kid. What the hell you need t' hang around with such bums for?"

And they go back in and sit all day waiting for the wheels of "justice" to grind their case to the top of the list. I've noticed something about cops and kids in court. When there is one cop and one kid, the cop almost always forgets things or otherwise behaves on the witness stand in a way that helps the kid. And the kid usually reciprocates by doing what the cop says he should do to get off and get the case over with.

But when there are two or more cops, or more than one kid, then the cops conspire and lie or do whatever they have to do to prove their superiority over the enemy.

It's like something I found out with the kids. When rival gangs or groups used to get set to fight, I would ask the leaders or the antagonists to come down into a basement and fight it out alone. They usually did and no one ever got hurt. They showed a lot of respect for each other, almost love when the thing was over, and made plans for the announcement of the results almost like you might imagine two heads of state planning a joint communique after a summit conference.

It's just another example to me of how street kids and cops are caught up in a net that's bigger than just them.

One day in a New York City courtroom, especially the youth parts, will convince even the most conservative among us that there is no justice for the poor. The courts with few exceptions have done almost as much to destroy a kid's belief in justice than any other institution except the public schools.

The courts are overcrowded. Too damn bad. A kid who is coming before a judge for the first time in his life, a kid whose freedom may be taken from him in a process that he neither trusts nor understands, can't be made to understand that he may end up in prison because the judge didn't have the time to give his case his full attention. And for most kids in jail that's the sad truth.

Judges have a lot of power and most of them use it badly. They take out their frustrations at having to sit so long with crowded court calendars on those with the least power. The young and the poor. People who appear before them in the most terror and with the least defense. Kids who get assigned to Legal Aid and have the benefit of maybe thirty seconds of consultation before their freedom goes up for grabs to be determined by the discretion (or the digestion) of a judge.

I've seen more racism that counts coming from judges than I have coming from cops. Maybe part of the difference between how I see cops and how I see judges comes from this. Cops are like an army, on a crusade, carrying out someone else's dirty work in a dirty way. But judges, they set standards, and by their administration of justice they also make policy. The police and the kids watch. They get their cues, their commitment to the existence of justice or the dominance of injustice from what they see and hear in the courtroom. It is hard to spend the day in a New York City courtroom without having the feeling when it's over that you have just come out of a sewer. There are exceptions to this, but they are becoming fewer and fewer.

Judges are supposed to be above the pettiness of the average man. That separation is, to me, what gives them the right to judge. They should be the human and intellectual elite. The best people we have in our communities. The people we trust the most. Impartial. Curious. Open-minded.

Instead, kids see men in black robes whose behavior is sometimes as base and crude as that of the most venomous bigot. And they don't know the open secret that many of these men got their judgeships the way a guy who wants to own his own cab gets his taxi medallion—on the open market. It's no secret that many judges got their jobs, not because of their wisdom or their knowledge or their impartiality, but through clubhouse politics. Money. Manipulation. And then they sit in judgment over a street kid who maybe had done someone out of a couple of bucks. Justice.

"In God We Trust" hangs over the bench in the Criminal Court.

Well, you gotta trust somebody.

The first time I was ever in a New York courtroom, I went with a sixteen year old who was arrested for taking part in a gang fight. A fight between a Puerto Rican and an Italian gang. None of the Italian kids were in court because none of them were arrested. Three of the Puerto Rican kids were snagged. The kid I was with, Carlos, sat nervously through the three hours before his case was finally called. When it was, we both nervously stood up and walked self-consciously down the middle aisle toward the judge, who, symbolically, it seemed, sat above the rest of us.

The kid was acquitted. Even the Legal Aid defense attorney was able to make mincemeat of the prosecution's case when it was made clear that no one on the other side was arrested, and that the arresting officer was Italian. The charges were dropped, and it seemed small dues to pay that we had to wait those three hours. My first view of New York justice might have been a good one, if the judge hadn't added his own bias into the picture, for no apparent reason and to no apparent good.

"This all happened on Thirteenth Street?" the judge asked menacingly.

"Yes sir," answered Carlos.

"Speak up, I can't hear you."

"Yes sir," answered Carlos much louder.

"Look at me when you answer me. Now what did you say?"

"Yes sir," Carlos answered loudly and looking at the judge.

"Well you go back and tell your people that they're going to have to stop this drinking beer and playing loud music and throwing their bottles and garbage in the streets so the good people can't live there anymore. Do you understand me? You go back and tell your people that."

Blam. It was like pulling the rug out from under me. All of a sudden I was at the capture of an Indian at a cavalry post in a bad Randolph Scott movie. The general was sending a redskin home to Cochise with a warning. Bad medicine. The wardrums would beat from such a humiliating challenge.

It was hard for me to look at Carlos all the way home.

Finally, when I did, I asked a clumsy question.

"What do you think he was really saying?"

"I guess he don't like Puerto Ricans," Carlos answered.

JUST GOT OUT OF THE CAGE
I LOOK UP TO THE BUILDING. THAT MY FRIEN
ONCE LIVED IN. MOST OF THEM ARE PRObEbLY
IN PRISON, IN THE HOSPITAL, ON STUFF, IN VIET
NAM, DRINKING WINE IN THE BOWERY, DEALING
DRUGS, OR DEAD.
COME TO THINK OF IT ONLY TWO
SURVIVED. TONY AND PAPO.
TONY GOT MARRIED AND WORKS IN A FACTORY
AND PAPO IS THE SUPER IN THIS MIDDLE
CLASS BUILDING.

   I WONDER WHERE I'll GO WHEN MY
bUILDING COMES DOWN. TO ANOTHER SLUM
I GUESS.
"SHIT, MAN" WHEN IS THIS ALL GONNA END.

The 100 Centre Street, boy, you better dress up neat blues

You speak English
Yes Sir.
Speak up. I can't hear you—
    You speak English
Yes Sir
Can you afford a lawyer
No Sir
OK. Legal Aid.
    Put him in
Next case

Stand up straight and take your hands
    out of your pocket
Yes Sir
Where's your family? Why isn't your family here?
My mother works
What's that? Speak up.
My mother works

Well doesn't she know that you're in
    serious trouble? We all work
    but doesn't she know she has an
    obligation to this court to be here?
Yes Sir
Well you can just wait. You go back and wait
    and we'll give your mother time to come
    Call the case later
But my mother's at work
Call the next case.

What is this? A sentence?
Yes your Honor
Any motions?
No your Honor. I'd just like to say the boy
    does have a job and this is his first offense
Shoplifting is theft Mr. Defense Attorney, are you
    aware of that
Yes Sir
Six months in the city prison
Call the next case.

About Evelyn

This was transcribed from a tape made by a sixteen year old who we will call "Mike" who came into LEAP one day and the kids fed him dinner. He asked if he could tell someone his story—if it could be recorded— almost like he was making out his will. After he was finished he left and we never saw him again.

It started about three or three and a half years ago. I met Evelyn. I guess I fell in love with her and she fell in love with me. We started going together. Our families didn't know each other at the beginning, then they became acquainted. Evelyn and I went to the same school and I walked her home every day. We got along very well. Her mother didn't mind at first that we saw each other so much; neither did my parents. After school I would walk her home. She lived near me.

I saw her a lot in the neighborhood, too. Then my parents saw us go to church on Sunday and I talked about her to them. Then I came to her house with permission from her mother.

Evelyn had eight brothers and an adopted sister. Her brothers liked me very much and still do. Most of them are now against me for what happened but they still like me. I went to her house after school and would go home about 6:00 P.M., eat dinner, and come back around 7:30 and stay until about 11:00 P.M. We would watch television or talk. Her mother would be there, too, and she would watch television with us or talk. She was pretty nice but in a way I did not like her. Her house was very messy and during lunch time she would give Evelyn money for lunch to eat in a restaurant. I didn't like this because the restaurant was awful, it was dirty and everybody there spoke pretty bad. I think her mother should have had food for Evelyn at home.

When I went to her house, her mother was pleasant but she had a lot of arguments with her son over a girl coming to the house. I always felt uncomfortable about this. Evelyn would also have a lot of arguments with her mother and then take it out on me, because she didn't have anybody else to take it out on. I would then, as we say today, eat up her mind and she would stop arguing with me and we would get on a different subject.

About a year and a half ago our problem really started. Her mother was tired of seeing me and she started telling my mother I was seeing the girl too much. My mother started on me calling the girl a tramp and saying she was no good. This got worse and worse. Then her mother became nasty and in many ways let me know she didn't want me at her house anymore. I went anyway.

Then I got tired of all this and started playing hooky so I could see my girl and we started meeting in different places. I had the key to my apartment; we would go up there. We did this about sixty-eight times that year and one day I really goofed. I forgot my father was off of work that day and had taken my sister to the hospital for shots. We came to the apartment about 10:00 A.M. and about 10:45 we were leaving the apartment when I heard the key going into the door and told her to hide in the closet. My father started arguing with me about why I was not in school. I lied and said I got sick at school and came home. He hung up his coat in the closet and found her. We were both very scared. All we ever did in the apartment was listen to records and talk. There was a lot of kissing but nothing else ever went on there. My father grabbed me, told us to sit down and she was so scared she ran out of the apartment. I ran after her and stopped her in the hallway. I asked her what she was going to do. She said she would not go home because her mother would beat her with an electric cord. Most of the Spanish mothers and fathers use a strap or something like that, but not her mother. I had seen the marks on her arms and legs from the electric cord before. She said she was going to run away from home.

I told Evelyn that it was very bad for me too and I did not want to lose her, but I didn't think we should run away. But I said I would leave home too because I knew of places where we could stay but she wouldn't be able to stay there without me. I went back into the apartment. My father saw me getting ready to leave and he grabbed me. I told him never to grab me again. Before I left my father told me he was going to tell her mother about this and he also said if I left I could never come back.

She and I left very mixed up about what to do. I knew we had to decide what to do. I knew there was a party, we call it a set, on Essex and Stanton that day. We got to the set about 12 o'clock and stayed until about 3:30. Everybody had to leave then because my friend's parents were coming home and everybody at the party was playing hooky.

We walked to 42nd Street and stayed there a long time looking in the windows trying to decide what to do. We got back down to 5th Street and Avenue D about 5:30. We went to my friend's house. I've known him about eight and one-half years and he's almost like my brother. We explained everything to him and asked him if we could stay in his apartment. We stayed there about two weeks. We slept in the same bed but nothing ever happened.

We went to see her sister-in-law and her sister-in-law persuaded us to go to her aunt. When we got to her aunt's her mother was there and we were caught. We could have run out but I did not want to do this. We were brought to the precinct because my mother and her mother took out a summons for us and we had to go to Children's Court.

I knew one of the detectives at the precinct and he let us go back home. The next day we went to court. We had a woman judge, her name was Lisa, and she seemed pretty pleasant at the beginning but rough at the end. She heard our story and our parents' story. She released us but warned us that the next time we would get a probation officer.

We were pretty relieved. Evelyn's mother sort of forgave me and allowed me to see her but her mother was more strict than before. My mother kept on saying the girl was no good. My father didn't talk much about the girl—he only cared that I stayed out of trouble. My mother was much more dominating than my father. As a matter of fact I saw this in a report in the court psychiatrist's office.

I got sick of my mother always talking about the girl and left home. The next day my girl looked for me all day long and she said she wouldn't go home unless I went with her. I said I wouldn't. I was sick of everybody talking—my family and her family. She said if I was leaving, she was leaving too. I finally said okay to this and we stayed at my friend's house for about three or four weeks. Then her mother saw her and back we went to the precinct. The same detective let us go home that night but we had to go to court the next day. The next day in court we both got a probation officer. I was on probation for six months to a year, and I would have to see my probation officer every two weeks. Evelyn had to do the same thing.

I was not allowed to go to her house any more but I would always see her on the outside. The arguments started all over again with my family and her family. The whole neighborhood seemed to know things about us that were not even true. My family and her family were telling everybody. I left home and she left home for the third time.

We got a furnished room and I started working on

Waverly Place in a factory. I would punch holes in raincaps. This paid very little, about $40 a week, but it was, as you say, some money for the pocket. We got sick of everything and she talked me into turning ourselves in. I called the 7th Precinct and talked to the detective who had been friendly before. I asked him if there was any way of going to Youth House without letting our parents know that night. He said yes, come in and fill out the papers. I said I would call him back in about fifteen minutes. We then called the admitting office at Youth House and asked them if we could go to Youth House without going to the precinct. They said no, a warrant would have to be made out for us to go to Youth House.

So we went to the precinct. I filled out all the papers which took a long time and a patrol car took us to Youth House and then they called our parents. We went to court the next day and had the same judge and she was fed up with us. She gave me thirty days and Evelyn thirty days in Youth House. . . .

It was very bad for me at the beginning at Youth House because I was new there and everybody had been there before. At the end of thirty days we went back to court and the same judge, Lisa, released me with two-years' probation. She sent Evelyn back for five months to Youth House.

I did my five months on probation and then Evelyn came out. I saw my parole officer every two weeks. He was always making speeches against Evelyn saying she was no good and that her family was no good. He kept telling me that I came from such a good family and that I was much too good for her. I listened to him but I got very aggravated. But I would just listen.

Evelyn was changed to Junior High School #71 and since she lived on Pitt Street it was a long way for her to go to school. I would meet her and walk her to school and then walk her half-way home from school. I would meet her when she could get out. This went on for a while but my mother found out I was seeing her and things got very rough. My probation officer found out I was seeing her too and told me to be careful or I would be in big trouble. I said we were doing nothing wrong. This went on every time I saw him. I could never understand this. We did nothing wrong and we were a real team together. My mother kept laying it on, arguing all the time about her and calling her a tramp.

One night while my mother was taking a bath and my father was sleeping I took $35 from my mother's wallet. About 2:30 in the morning I left the house. I knew I couldn't stay at home. I went to my friend's house that night and Evelyn came over the next day. We were going to leave for Baron, Georgia. I had a friend there who was also just like a brother to me. He had a place there. He was in the army and had a kid but I knew we would be safe there. The tickets to get there cost $50 and all we had was $35. So we had to stay home until I could save the rest.

We stayed at my friend's house but after a while we got a furnished room. I didn't have a job so we had to start using the $35. I had to depend on my friends for money. We would eat at different friends' apartments. I never took anything without paying for it and I never asked for anything. We stayed in the furnished room for about three weeks. This was the fourth time we had run away. We got very tired of this. One night we started walking. We walked to First Avenue between 2nd and 3rd Street.

I went to see my aunt. She was not too mad at me but she called my mother up. My mother came with three police officers with a warrant. The officers said she could tear up the warrant right there and everything would be forgotten. But my mother said no, I want to see him inside.

I was pushed into a police car with my parents there. Evelyn went home and begged her mother not to turn her in because the court was looking for her. Her mother said okay. She would hide her from the court.

I got a month and a half in the Youth House. I was now used to the routine there and got along pretty well. In fact, I still have the telephone number of my supervisor there. The supervisors there were more or less on my side. They would even go to my neighborhood during the day and come back and tell me what was going on. I even had the privilege of using the telephone at Youth House and we weren't supposed to have this privilege.

After a month and a half in Youth House I went back to court and was released on probation. I had a different judge this time. The court asked me where Evelyn was and I told them I didn't know. I really didn't know that she was home and that her mother was hiding her from the court. My probation was reduced to six months. In a way I was now safe and she was running.

One night her mother argued with her and threatened to turn her in. Evelyn came to me with this story. So I left home again for the fifth time. I found a place in Brooklyn and everything was okay but I was very broke. Friends of mine paid the rent but we needed money. Again Evelyn said let's turn ourselves in and forget about everything. She talked me into it and I was put in for a month and a half this time. I was sure I would be sent upstate this time, and not stay at Youth House. I put on an act at Youth House and said I had a toothache. They don't have a dentist there so they took me to a dentist in the Bronx and I escaped.

I went home and begged my mother not to send me back. I stayed home for two days but my parents decided to take me to court on Monday. I had a Negro judge this time who really thought I was crazy. The judge said, "I can't let you go. You escaped from Youth House and you will have to go back for three days until your hearing is due." I thought I would be able to go home from court but they sent me to Youth House right from court. I was really mad about that. I went back to Youth House for three days.

I was released after the hearing but Evelyn wasn't. She came out on a pass and when she saw me she wanted us to run away again. I said no. She said she would go alone then. Since I was so involved I finally left with her again. This was the sixth time we ran away.

We went to my friend's house again for a while but then we got a furnished room. Her mother and brother caught her on the street and we were sent to Youth House again. I was sent there now for two months. The judge said there was only one thing left to do. He said I would have to go to a place upstate called Lincoln Hall in Westchester, New York. It was a training school for boys run by the Catholic Brothers. From what they said about it, it sounded all right. I was to leave for there Monday.

On Saturday before I left there was a dance in Youth

House and I saw Evelyn there. She was getting released on Monday and I was leaving for Lincoln Hall on Monday. I was very happy for her.

I had been told that I would be at Lincoln Hall from four to six months but when I told the people this at Youth House they laughed at me. They said nobody gets out of Lincoln Hall before at least eighteen months.

I went to Lincoln Hall and hated it. I did go to school there. Every Sunday my parents visited me and I told them how much I hated it. Everything had to be done to perfection or you would have your privileges taken away from you, or you would be smacked around. We were allowed a cigarette every forty-five minutes and this was one of the things that was taken away if you didn't do everything to perfection. My parents didn't listen to me.

I decided to be bad and start bad right away. I was so bad I was thrown into solitary. Solitary there is pretty awful. All you do is stay in bed with no clothes on. Sometimes if they don't feel like giving you food in solitary, they don't. It was freezing there too and on top of that they turn on a fan.

After being in solitary, the Brother came in and asked me if I had thought about it. I said yes and he let me out. I hated it all the more.

Two others felt the same way about Lincoln Hall as I did. We decided to escape on a Thursday. There are lots of woods and mountains up there and we ran through the woods. They were pretty rough to get through and the other two wanted to get onto the road. I told them if we did that we would get caught. But they did it anyway and they did get caught. I ran through the woods so fast that I did about twenty-five miles in three hours. I was so tired and figured that I was far enough away so that I could go onto the road.

Fortunately a man in a car picked me up. I gave him a big B.S. story. I said I was going into Manhattan and he said he would drive me. He drove me to the Tri-borough Bridge. I walked for about a mile and was so tired that I caught a taxi to 59th Street and the West Side. When we got there I reached into my pocket like I was getting out my wallet and opened the door and ran out. I ran into a train station and ducked under the rails and came down to 5th Street.

After being here for about two weeks I saw Evelyn. She is now a lesbian. She dresses like one in boy's clothes and has a boy's haircut. She goes with a girl that I knew was a lesbian in Youth House. I heard that her mother said if she sees me she is going to turn me in.

A sick day in a sick man's life

Man I got up sick this morning. It took a lot of hours before I got a fix yesterday, man. I hope I'm lucky today. I don't think I could go through the same shit today. I got to think of some fucking way of getting some bread but fast, before I start with the motherfucking chills again. That's some goddam shit for me to be going through. Dig, maybe I could borrow a few bucks. No, that's bullshit. Every fucking guy I know is going through this same shit. The motherfuckers who have the money won't lend it to me. Someday they'll come to me for a fix. They're going to kiss my ass.

I better start looking for ways to get some dough. Maybe I could get me a battery or something from a fucking car or beat the shit out of a motherfucking dealer and take his stuff and money. He don't need it half as bad as I do. . . . Man, I'll have to be cool. The man almost caught me last time. Those white motherfuckers had to come to their car just as I had the fucking battery in my hand. White bastard.

Oh man, I feel terrible. My brain's busting inside. My motherfucking head, my stomach—it feels like it's getting ripped apart. Oh God, help me—please, please help me, Goddam. I'm getting chills and nauseous. Man it's cold. Oh God, please help me.

I better make it before the cops come—I didn't want to hit that fucking old man, but I need my fix. I hope I didn't kill him. Fuck him. Nobody told him to be showing his lousy money. Oh God, finally. I got my fix after all this motherfucking time. This should kick the pains for a while. Man, in this little fucking bag there is a miracle worker. The little old Life Restorer. All the motherfucking trouble I got getting it—but it finally pays off. Man any motherfucking minute I'll feel like the King of the World. Yeah, man—this is the life, not a fucking worry in The World. Man I feel good. This is the best high I ever had.

Shit no! I don't give a fuck what those motherfuckers are staring at. Fucking people don't give me a motherfucking thing. They're staring at me like I'm some sort of freak—I'm just as good as they are. Fuck their staring anyway, I don't owe them a fucking thing.

I'm O.K. Man, I'm still awake—no, I'm alright. I told you, I'm not asleep.

I'm alright I'm alright I'm alright—not a worry in the world.

The visit

Who's there?

Mr. Goldberg, your investigator.

Hold on, please. I'm not dressed.

Jose, get up! The investigator is outside. Get dressed and go down the fire escape. Victor, Carlos, Mike, David, Danny, Mary! Hurry up! The investigator is here. Mary, get your father's clothes out of here. David, put the phone under the couch. The rest of you hide the T.V. Listen. He's gonna ask you how come you're not in school. Tell him the truth, how you got no school clothes and no shoes and there's no hot water to take a bath.

Goddamn. What's that motherfucker doing here so early? It's only 8:00 in the fucking morning.

You know those motherfuckers can come any old time and Mom lets them in.

They come early in the morning just to spy on us and Mom has to take that shit.

Good morning, Mr. Goldberg.

Good morning. I came to pay you a visit like I said. Am I disturbing anything?

No, no, you're not.

What are the children doing here? Aren't they attending school?

Like I told you yesterday, my kids don't have enough shoes or clothes. I need money to buy them clothes.

I'm sorry, we don't give money anymore for clothing.

Hey! Did you hear what he said? We can't get no damn school clothes. Shit. If we work, man, they cut Mom's money. If we don't we're screwed anyway. He should live here! 67 cents a day ain't even enough to buy food and he wants us to buy clothes.

I don't understand Mom. She tells us to hide what we have. Shit, there's nothing to hide.

I'm lucky I'm working. We can have a phone and some food. If they find out, man, Mom gets fucked up. I don't understand this fucking government. They say that they're spending too much money on Welfare. Where the fuck is all the money?

They're spending money killing Viet Cong and shooting faggots to the moon, while we're down here starving. Ain't this supposed to be the richest country in the world?

I guess so?!!

Hey man, diy him checking out the rooms.

Come in.

Good morning kids. Did I awaken you?

Nah. We don't sleep, we're freaks.

How many people are sleeping in this room?

Can't you see? How many beds you see, man? Four beds, right? Six kids! All in one room, real cozy, man.

It's not my fault, young man!

I don't want to hear it, man! It's our fault, right. Our father cut out and our mother can't work so you stick us in a dump and you say you're helping us.

I'm tired of you people. We're not animals, we're human too. You come early in the morning and start searching the fucking place. I'm tired of your shit, man! If I had my way I wouldn't open the door! But my mother thinks she needs you.

How can you say that. I'm trying to help you young man!

Mighty funny, big help you motherfuckers are!

Good morning, sorry I disturbed you.

Don't come back here so early next time mother-fucker or I'll kick you out. I can take care of my own family.

Fuck you, Welfare Man! Keep your money.

Shit. I hope sis don't turn out to be like Mom.

Naa, Carlos, she's pretty slick. It's only Puerto Rican mothers who come off fresh from the banana boat who get fucked up by whitey. I'll tell you something, man, even the mothers are getting fed up with being pushed around by school teachers, principals, landlords, wel-fare people, cops, and everybody.

Man, one of these days mothers are going to fight back. But I think they're going to have to learn from us.

Shit!

What whitey would let some stranger poke around in their fucking underwear?

Powerlessness and antidotes

Street kids are powerless. All their violent, self-destructive, and antisocial actions are an attempt to come to grips with that lack of power, because no one willingly accepts imposed impotence. Especially not in a society that makes such a fetish of power.

Street kids know they have none of it. Even less than other kids, because most of them can't count on their families *at all* to insulate them, never mind the dues middle-class kids must pay for it. I'm not talking about power in any ideological way. Just the kind of force or strength it takes to be free and to prevent you from being exploited by everyone. That's all I mean. Street kids are powerless, and even their fumbling attempts at warfare just serve to prove that in the end when they lose.

For as long as I can remember, street kids have immortalized their impotence by being tatooed with a three-word inscription. It usually happens coincidental with joining the junkie ranks. It reads "BORN TO LOSE." And they ought to know.

The racial and economic conditions that have created this absence of power in the young, the black, and the poor are not going to change in any important way during the lives of the kids now living on the streets. Evolutionary changes, if they are going to come at all, will come too late. So if the kids of the streets are to be saved from further and growing disasters, somebody is going to have to do something not evolutionary. Revolutionary.

Some entirely new form must be created out of the resources at hand. A new form that will compensate for the lack of power of the young, giving them the time and the motivation to grow up whole.

LEAP is a beginning. Adults and kids living and working together on problems common to all of them. Setting up that big family again. The kind bullies leave alone. Working ways out of the minefield and working out ways to live in it. Big city communes. People taking over old buildings and making them live again. Places to live, to learn, to have fun.

Or maybe other ways. Groups of people who have some warmth and strength to give and who want some warmth and strength in return, becoming advocates for kids on a certain street, or two or three. People kids can call when they're in trouble and alone and who will listen to them, hear them, and be prepared to go out of their way for them. Not a profession, but people. People willing to let children be children. What this means is a group of friends getting to know a younger group of friends. It will, at first, be artificial. But then, any immunization is artificial. It will be stiff and uncomfortable. Groping around for ways to make contact. Making mistakes and saying wrong things. Not knowing the language. But the truth of it, the honesty of it will make up for all of that after the first time the bridge is used. And it will become apparent quickly that the bridge will be used in both directions.

But the bridges need to be built and we can't afford to give the job to the same old architects, because they don't design them so the two ends ever come together. They just build nice looking approach ramps to the cliffs. I think we should tear up our contracts with those people and try building our own.

Spinning off of LEAP, we've begun to put a lot of those kid-adult groups together across the country. The Institute for Juvenile Justice has been traveling around the U.S. helping local communities establish contact with their own kids on their own streets. Helping advocacy groups spring up in opposition to the destructive systems kids are now facing alone. Local Institutes take on their own character and work on their own unique problems. All that ties them together is their mutual belief in the rights of children to live free from fear and exploitation. There is no national bureaucratic chain. Just a national catalyst to bring people together and educate them to their real resources and potential. Educating people not to give their proxies away so easily in behalf of the kids on their streets and to carefully examine the proxies already given.

The Institute for Juvenile Justice has its bases in Alburquerque, New Mexico and New York City. Local groups have started in San Francisco, Denver, and New Orleans. Lawyers working out legal procedures to prevent the institutional destruction of kids from the streets. People interested in education working out their ideas for new kinds of schools free from force and intimidation. Business people looking for ways to use the energy and vitality that is wasted when kids are. People looking for answers. Kids looking for a union. The same kind of negotiating power that other "special interest groups" have.

The Institute represents part of the exciting beginning of a new realignment of power. No more swallowing whole the pessimism of those who need to justify their failures. Just a lot of people who aren't afraid of their streets or their kids or each other. I hope they spring up everywhere. In every city, large or small where kids are left to the streets and the fates.